ISIS: Race to Armageddon

ISIS: Race to Armageddon

By
Dr. Adil Rasheed

(Established 1870)

United Service Institution of India

New Delhi

Vij Books India Pvt Ltd

New Delhi (India)

Published by

Vij Books India Pvt Ltd
(Publishers, Distributors & Importers)
2/19, Ansari Road
Delhi – 110 002
Phones: 91-11-43596460, 91-11-47340674
Fax: 91-11-47340674
e-mail: vijbooks@rediffmail.com

ISBN   : 978-93-84464-77-6 (Hardback)
ISBN   : 978-93-85563-07-2 (Paperback)

Paperback edition published in 2016

English Translation of the Arabic text on the Cover is "*The Islamic State of Iraq*", followed by the ISIS motto "*Enduring*"

To God and Mom

Contents

Acknowledgments

There are many to whom I owe profound thanks and gratitude for their guidance, help and assistance in the writing of this book. First, I would like to earnestly thank Almighty God for having showered His blessings upon me every moment of my life. I am also deeply grateful to my mother, Ms Zubaida Khan, for her love, care and support through all the trials and travails and to my father, the Late Major Abid Rasheed (May his soul rest in peace).

I am immensely grateful to the United Service Institution of India (USI) for the wealth of intellectual profundity and strategic insight I gained as Senior Research Fellow in this most esteemed and illustrious research centre of India.

It would not have been possible for me to conduct a study of such critical importance to global security without the keen guidance and support I received from the Director of the USI, Lieutenant General PK Singh, PVSM, AVSM (Retd). His intellectual calibre, profound insights and gracious encouragement proved vital in the successful completion of this research.

I cannot thank enough my true mentor in this project, Major General BK Sharma, AVSM, SM** (Retd), who guided me at every step on the way with his astute knowledge and insights, wise counsel and unflinching support. I would also like to particularly thank Major General PK Goswami, VSM (Retd) for lending his support and valuable insights to me during the course of this project.

A very special mention here is for Dr Roshan Khanijo, who stood by me as a friend, philosopher and guide on a daily basis throughout the course of this study. I would also like to thank the sincere friendship and guidance I received from all the researchers and colleagues at the USI, with whom I discussed and gained insights on several aspects of the subject. I would like to especially thank Commodore Lalit Kapur (Retd), Group Captain Sharad Tewari, VM (Retd), Colonel Rohit Mehrotra, Colonel SK Shahi, Colonel Sanjeev Relia and indeed Commander MH Rajesh for their invaluable contributions that are too many to be fully acknowledged and thanked. I would also like to thank my other friends at the USI — Naib Subedar Sube Singh, Havaldar Dharambir Singh, Lance Naik Inderjeet Singh, Ms Aparna Roy, Surendra Kumar Tiwari and Rajesh Kumar.

I would also like to mention here the help and support I received from some of my friends and associates outside my place of work. I would like to particularly thank Shweta Desai, Associate Fellow at the Centre for Land Warfare Studies, New Delhi, for her valuable insights and suggestions. I am deeply grateful to Mr P. Ramesh Kumar at Bennett, Coleman and Co. Ltd. (Times Group) for his friendship and genuine support, as well as to my steadfast friends Mr. Ehtesham Shahid, Mr. Mohammed Shiraz and Abdul Naseeb Khan. I have also been very fortunate in receiving support from various research scholars and strategic experts living in West Asia, particularly Dr Ahmed Menassi and Dr Farid Azzi from the Emirates Center for Strategic Studies and Research, based in the UAE.

Finally, I would especially like to thank my dear wife Afiya Khan for her love, patience and encouragement and for taking full care of my lovely children, Yousuf and Mariam, even as I was busy writing the book. I dedicate this humble work to my countrymen and to the cause of peace and harmony in the world.

– **Dr. Adil Rasheed**
May 2015

Preface : Black Flags of Apocalypse!

When experts on terrorism first declared the ISIS as more dangerous than Al-Qaeda, it seemed an outrageous claim. Many wondered how the very superlative of extremism and terror could be placed below an upstart group in the comparative degree. But the claim did not take long to validate itself. It was explained that the ISIS is not only richer than Al-Qaeda, but is arguably the richest terrorist organization in human history. The rapidity with which the ISIS forces won territories in Iraq and Syria increased its strength by the hundreds of thousands, thus underscoring the disturbing fact that the group had far more militants than the few thousands that Al-Qaeda could muster even at its peak. But then came the barbarity, the like of which the world had never seen, in that it was even more gruesome than that of Al-Qaeda. Videos of the beheadings and burnings of innocent hostages became part of the ISIS' perverse public relations campaign to attract global sociopaths to its grotesque cause. In addition, the group openly claimed to be fomenting sectarian violence and ethnic cleansing in Iraq and Syria as part of its 'nikaya' program — a strategy of brutally hurting the enemy in order to undermine stability in both countries. In its online magazine *Dabiq*, ISIS brazenly justified indulging in sex trade and the destruction of the ancient cities of Nimrud and Patra. But these atrocities were nothing compared to its larger design and objective of obliterating nation states (in principle and in practice) in order to establish its dystopian version of a global Caliphate.

But perhaps the greatest threat that has made the ISIS more problematic for global security than Al-Qaeda is its bloodlust and program to instigate a global apocalyptic war between Islam and the West in order to justify its claim of being the Caliphate. The US President Obama came close to properly identifying the ISIS by calling it as a death cult. In fact, the ISIS is more than that. It is a doomsday cult, which is bent on bringing about the the Biblical Armageddon (what it calls in Arabic as 'Al-Malhama

Al-Kubra') in our age. This level of ideological perversity and madness has been characterised as the third generation of global jihad, or Terror 3.0 by former CIA Director General Michael Hayden.

This book highlights the ISIS' plans to initiate 'Total Confrontation' with the world from 2016-2020 as part of its 'Masterplan' detailed in the book by Fouad Huseein titled: '*Second Generation of Al-Qaeda*' by attacking the city of Rome and the Vatican, in order to begin a global inter-religious war. Unlike Al-Qaeda, Iraq is central to its global jihadist aspirations for the ISIS. It follows Al-Zarqawi's thinking of waging and winning a jihad in Iraq as central because "if jihad fails in Iraq, the [Muslim] nation will never rise again."[1]

Chapter One of this book focuses on the phoenix-like rise of the ISIS on the global stage in 2014 after its virtual elimination following the death of the dreaded Abu Mus'ab Al-Zarqawi in Iraq in 2006. Chapter Two tracks the growth of political Islam or Islamism in the 19th and 20th centuries, and how its concepts grew distinct from the teachings of mainstream Islam, leading to the Jihadist ideology of Al-Qaeda and the ISIS.

Chapter Three is dedicated to the organization of the ISIS and Chapter Four to the warfare of the terror group and the way it has incorporated and implemented novel strategies of barbarity expounded by post-9/11 jihadi ideologues of Al-Qaeda.

Chapter Five describes how the ISIS has effectively spread its message and built its bases around the world in less than a year and has proven to be ahead of the proverbial curve when it comes to spreading its propaganda on the Internet and in conducting cyber warfare.

It also looks into the strong renunciation of the global Muslim community of the ISIS ideology and its violent atrocities and makes a few recommendations on the measures countries like India should take in order to fight the growing global menace of ISIS' extremism and terrorism. This book has used the appellation ISIS simply because it is the most popular name of the group in the world and because it finds the moniker 'Islamic State' as unacceptable to describe the group, as it is neither Islamic or a state in any which way.

Chapter One
Introduction: The Genesis of ISIS

Picture of an ISIS militant on horseback featuring on ISIS online magazine
Dabiq

"The spark has been lit here in Iraq, and its heat will continue to intensify ...
until it burns the Crusader armies."

Abu Mus'ab Al-Zarqawi
(Putative Father of the ISIS)

1.   Rise to Global Infamy

In June 2014, a breakaway faction of Al-Qaeda with a newly minted moniker — the Islamic State of Iraq and Syria (ISIS) — grabbed global media spotlight for capturing vast swathes of the Iraqi Sunni heartland. The world was shocked by the lightning advance of this extremist group, which with less than a thousand marauders[2] seized roughly a third of Iraqi and Syrian territories by the middle of August[3]. The 'four to five divisions'[4] (with 30,000 to 50,000 soldiers)[5] of the US-trained Iraqi Army put up little to no resistance, with many of its soldiers deserting their posts, stripping their uniforms and leaving much of the weaponry and sophisticated military hardware behind.

The explosive expansion and extreme brutality of this summer offensive, catapulted the ISIS to global infamy. Clearly, the implications of this largely unforeseen development resonated beyond the territories ISIS seized in Iraq and Syria and the consequences of the establishment of its so-called Caliphate might outlast the eventual decimation of this terrorist organization and its fledgling proto-state.

For one, the ISIS' sudden emergence on the geopolitical stage and its threat to upset the whole post-Ottoman regional shebang by obliterating the boundaries of nation states (as exemplified by it in Iraq and Syria) in order to reinstate a medieval theocratic empire has shocked the global political system. Various international organizations, government agencies and media outlets remain baffled to this day over the modus operandi and warfare that has led to the ISIS' spectacular success.

Several causes have been attributed to the rise of the ISIS. The most important of them was the US-led Iraq War of 2003, which destroyed the state of Iraq and led to its virtual trifurcation along sectarian lines.

As a result of the war, Baghdad came under the dominance of the Shiite marsh Arabs for the first time in Islamic history, as the Sunnis of Iraq were completely sidelined from the power equation. The perceived sectarian policies of the Maliki regime and its inability to check the violence perpetrated by Shiite militias against the Sunni community forced the marginalized Sunni tribes to support extremist jihadist groups of Al-Qaeda and ISIS in Iraq.

The unease of Sunni Gulf monarchs, in the wake of rising Shiite influence in Iraq, the Levant, Yemen and even in Gulf countries, led them to support Salafi jihadist militias in Syria and Iraq.

The large-scale civil war and violence perpetrated by the Syrian regime of Bashar Al-Assad to quell the country's democratic forces of the Syrian National Coalition (particularly the Free Syrian Army) proved helpful for Islamist groups to gain ground in Syria and Iraq, mainly Al-Qaeda and the ISIS.[6]

The US decision to withdraw from Iraq before completing its promised nation-building and its inability to take a tough stance against the Syrian regime were instrumental in the rise of the ISIS and Jabhat Al Nusrah.

The disbanding of the Iraq army and the widespread resentment among former Baathist soldiers, along with the large-scale unemployment of youth and the failure of the Arab Spring facilitated the rise of the radical Sunni jihadism in Iraq and Syria.

2.   Vision and Motto

The ISIS follows an eschatological variant of Salafi-jihadist school of Sunni Islam and employs terrorism in the name of jihad (condemned by most Islamic scholars as religiously proscribed) by targeting all non-Muslim and most Muslim communities under the doctrine of 'takfeer' (which legitimizes killing of people after declaring them infidels), as part of its global campaign to "purge" Muslim-dominated countries and then the world for restoring its version of a theocratic Caliphate.

The group's motto is 'Baqiyya wa Tamaddad,' which means 'Enduring and Expanding'.[7] It controls vast swathes of territory in Sunni-dominated regions of Syria and Iraq, a stretch larger in area than the United Kingdom[8].

The city of Raqqa (in Syria) is considered to be the administrative center of the ISIS and Mosul in Iraq is the largest city in its grip.

The Logo of the ISIS is purportedly borrowed from the Seal of the Prophet. The message on the ISIS' black standard is Islam's first article of faith (the 'Shahadah' or Testimony). It reads: "There is no God Except *The* God and Muhammad is His Messenger"

The group also claims to be holding territories in Egypt, Algeria, Saudi Arabia, Yemen Afghanistan and Pakistan. However since January 2015, ISIS has reportedly lost about 5,000 to 6,000 square miles of territory, according to Pentagon sources.[9]

There has been about 25 percent reduction in the areas under its control in Iraq. In early April 2015, ISIS was expelled from the city of

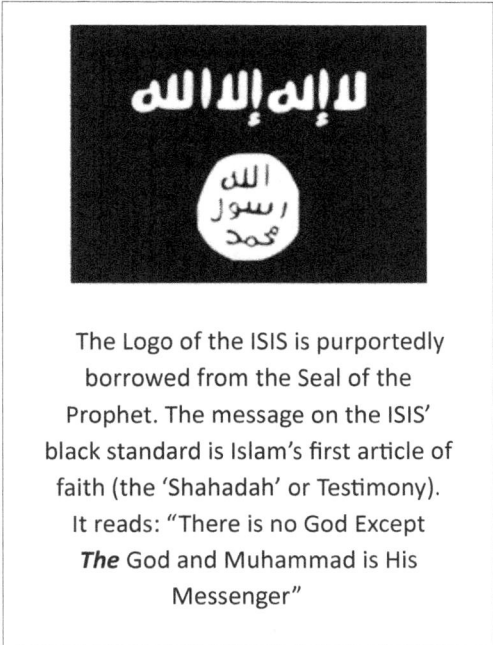

Saddam Hussein's birth, Tikrit, by Iraqi government forces and the US-led coalition's airstrikes.

However, the ISIS managed to seize control of the strategically important city of Ramadi in Al-Anbar province and was reportedly advancing toward Iraq's biggest oil refinery in Baiji.

3. Significance of the ISIS Threat

The threat posed by the ISIS to global peace and security can hardly be overstated. ISIS poses a threat to the entire global community, including the Muslims of the world.

While announcing US-led global campaign against the ISIS on September 10, 2014, US President Barack Obama rightly observed: "ISIL (ISIS) poses a threat to the people of Iraq and Syria, and the broader Middle East ... If left unchecked, these terrorists could pose a growing threat beyond that region."

He added "ISIL is not 'Islamic'. No religion condones the killing of innocents, and the vast majority of ISIL's victims have been Muslim."[10] For his part, the Saudi Grand Mufti Sheikh Abdulaziz Al Sheikh has called the ISIS, "the number one enemy of Islam."[11]

Several factors have contributed to the emergence of the ISIS as a major threat to global political order and for being deemed as more dangerous than Al-Qaeda. First, by running over the Iraq-Syria border, the ISIS has sought to erase not only the boundaries of the two countries (as first established by the West under the Sykes-Picot agreement), but in doing so it categorically declared its repudiation of the Westphalian concept of the nation-state.

The ISIS then called itself the seed Caliphate, instituted on its own ultra-extremist, non-orthodox interpretation of Islam that does not conform to any of the four orthodox juristic schools of Sunni Islam, let alone of other Muslim sects. It also announced a five-year plan of expanding its boundaries to all Muslim-majority countries and beyond by building a legion to conduct a mythical end-time war between the West and Islam.[12]

Second, the so-called Islamic State has amassed enormous wealth and resources, greater than any terrorist or insurgent group in human history and has used it to expand its operations around the world. Third, the ISIS has developed its own jihadist mythology by concocting vague eschatological claims (as if to gain legitimacy on the basis of religious prophecy) through dubious and ambiguous reinterpretations of end-time predictions found in Hadeeth literature. In the words of US Army General Martin Dempsey, chairman of the joint-chiefs-of-staff, "This is an organisation that has an apocalyptic, end-of-days strategic vision which will eventually have to be defeated.[13]

Fourth, the organization has been able to win over followers and converts from across the world and from various national, ethnic and religious affiliations with the help of a powerful social media campaign.

Thus, it has attracted over 20,000 fighters from over 90 countries, according to the International Centre for the Study of Radicalization and Political Violence (February 2015).[14] Its total force strength is said to be in excess of 200,000. This is a much larger number than any jihadist or terrorist organization till date.

The organization is also said to rule over an area of the size of Britain. Thus, the threat posed by the ISIS to global security has in a short time emerged as far greater than that of Al-Qaeda.[15]

The fighters of the ISIS include foreign migrants, former soldiers of the Baathist regime of Saddam Hussein and the poor and disposed Sunni youth in Iraq and Syria, who have suffered a steep decline in their standard of living over the tumultuous years of the last decade.

"ISIS is the Number One Enemy of Islam"

Saudi Grand Mufti Sheikh Abdulaziz Al Sheikh

The foreign fighters are generally well-educated and come from middle-class, even upper middle-class families of Europe and Asia, many of whom are engineers, doctors, lawyers and PhDs.

Former members of the Baathist regime are generally soldiers and former high-ranking officials, who suffered the most following the US-led invasion and occupation of Iraq in 2003, and who bear deep resentment against US-led coalition forces and the Iraqi regime following the disbanding of Saddam's military as part of the de-Baathification program of the new political dispensation. Their military expertise and knowledge of warfare in the region have greatly benefitted the ISIS and many of the former Baathist military personnel, like the now deceased Haji Bakr, played a pivotal role in the rapid rise of ISIS in recent years.

The third group of ISIS fighters belong to the poor and dispossessed Sunni Iraqis who joined the group, either through conviction of belief and/or compulsion of circumstance.

4.   Morphing Identities, Changing Names

Till date, there remains a lot of confusion and mystery surrounding many aspects of the ISIS – its secret patrons and benefactors, its modus operandi and highly adaptive style of warfare, the size and composition of its forces and even its actual influence and control over territories.

The confusion extends to the very name and identity of the group, which was known by several names in the past and even today is called by different appellations, as the ISIS, ISIL, DA'ISH or by its latest self-proclaimed moniker "the Islamic State" (abbreviated as IS). It is ironic that the group's new acronym, when read as a word underscores this ontological confusion.

This book has used the acronym ISIS (Islamic State of Iraq and Al-Sham) for the group, simply because it is the most popularly known acronym associated with the group, and has been in vogue ever since it first came into global media spotlight with the capture of Mosul in June 2014.

In fact, it is not uncommon to find criminal and terrorist organizations deliberately having a number of names and aliases. By

The Arab world has stuck to the acronym DA'ISH for ISIS. DA'ISH is the Arabic abbreviation for Al-Dawla al-Islamiya fi al-Iraq wa al-Sham (the Islamic State of Iraq and Al-Sham). It purportedly has a derogatory connotation in the Arabic language as it implies a bigot who enforces his views.

THE BRIGAND OF BAGHDAD

ISIS Head Abu Bakr Al-Baghdadi

Born in Samarrah (Iraq) as Ibrahim Awad Ibrahim Al-Badri, the so-called 'Caliph Ibrahim' has a reward of upto $10m for information leading to his capture or death.

A lover of football in his teens, the reclusive Baghdadi is also nicknamed 'The Invisible Sheikh'. A Ph.D. in Islamic Studies from the Islamic University of Baghdad, he was interned by the US in Camp Bucca (2004).

Baghdadi got seriously injured in a raid led by US-led coalition on March 18, 2015, and Iranian Radio has even claimed that he has succumbed to his injuries and died. Before getting injured, it is rumored that Baghdadi married a German teenager.

constantly changing their identities, criminal and insurgent groups seek to operate in secret and remain intractable for their opponents. Therefore, it is only natural that the ISIS has changed its name several times in recent years.[16] On several occasions, the change was ostensibly brought about by a merger with or separation from other jihadi groups, while sometimes it simply added the names of its newly acquired territories, or areas it aspired to take control of in its title.

The group's earliest incarnation can be traced back to 1999, when Abu Musab Al-Zarqawi founded the Jamat-al-Tawheed-wal-Jihad (JTJ), translated as the "Organization of Monotheism and Jihad".

In 2004, the group took on the title 'Tanzim Qaidat al-Jihad fi Bilad al-Rifidadayn' (The Organization of Jihad's Base in the Country of the Two Rivers), but was then more commonly known as Al-Qaeda in Iraq (AQI). It merged into the Majlis al Shura al Mujahideen (MSM) in 2006 and after its virtual decimation by 2009, re-emerged as the Islamic State of Iraq (ISI) in 2013.

Then in April of 2014, the ISI renamed itself as the Islamic State of Iraq and Al-Sham (the ISIS) and after declaring itself as the Caliphate in June that year it called itself the Islamic State (the IS), in keeping with its pan-Islamist and globalist ambitions.

For their part, various governments and media outlets around the world also added to the confusion by naming the group differently. After its capture of the Iraqi city of Mosul, most governments and international organizations used to call the terror group Islamic State of Iraq and Syria (ISIS), as its area of influence spread across the countries referred to in the name.

However, there was disagreement over whether the word 'Al-Sham' in the Arabic full form of ISIS could be correctly translated as modern-day Syria because that word referred to the historical Syria, or what the French knew as the 'Levant' and reflected the ISIS' aspiration to take that whole region under its control.

Therefore, the United States as well as a few other countries have preferred to use the abbreviation ISIL (Islamic State of Iraq and the Levant) as the more appropriate name of the group.[17]

Meanwhile, the Arab world stuck to the acronym DA'ISH - the Arabic abbreviation of the group's original name, which can be transliterated as Al-Dawlat al-Islamiya fi al-Iraq wa al-Sham[18] (the English translation being the Islamic State of Iraq and Al-Sham).

The Arabic abbreviation DA'ISH when joined and read as a word in Arabic has a derogatory connotation in that language, as it is known to mean a bigot who enforces his views on others. It is for this reason that many Arab detractors of the ISIS started using the word 'Da'ish' to insult the group and in response the ISIS prohibited the use of the word and punished those who uttered it. In February, 2015, the ISIS reportedly (according to the newspaper *Daily Mail*) flogged a boy 60 times in a town square for calling the terror group 'Da'ish'.[19]

In fact, when it declared itself as the seed Caliphate in June 2014, the ISIS removed the words 'Iraq' and 'Al-Sham' from its full version Arabic name and simply became 'Dawlat-al-Islam' (transliterated), which can be translated into English as the 'Islamic State'. The new name attempts to underscore the group's transnational approach and reiterates its emphasis of being both quintessentially 'Islamic' as well as a full-fledged 'State'. It is an attempt to emphasize that the group is not being limited to just Iraq and 'Al-Sham' (or Levant) but has global territorial ambitions, which is presently seen with its occupation of some territories in Libya and Nigeria.

However, most international organizations continue to refrain from using the name 'Islamic State' or the abbreviation 'IS' as the legitimate name of the group because it gives the wrong impression that the areas under the ISIS' control are the territories of a new found 'state', and that its form of draconian governance is in any way related to Islam.

In September 2014, the French government announced that it would use the derogatory Arabic acronym DA'ISH as the name of the militant group, instead of ISIL (which it previously used).[20] Curiously, the word Levant that is represented as 'L' in the abbreviation ISIL is of French origin, but because of its colonial association the country chose to discard the abbreviation 'ISIL'. Meanwhile, the US Government continues to officially call the group as ISIL.

Similarly, some major English news agencies - such as Reuters, the Associated Press, Agence France-Press and Al-Jazeera – have opted to call the group the 'Islamic State in Iraq and Levant' or 'ISIL'. Others like the *New York Times* have persisted with the 'Islamic State in Iraq and Syria' (and in some cases Greater Syria).

However, several news agencies like the *Guardian*[21] and *Financial Times*[22] appear confused as they use the full form as 'Islamic State in Iraq and Levant' but opt for the acronym ISIS.

For its part, the BBC uses the recent variant, i.e. Islamic State or IS[23]. The confusion even exists in the non-English European media. In Spain, the newspaper *El Pais* calls the group El Estado Islámico en Irak y el Levante (EIIL). However, its rival newspaper *El Mundo* has gone with the name 'El Estado Islámico en Irak y el Syria', and uses the English acronym ISIS.

In Germany, *Deutsche Welle* uses ISIS in both English and German versions but writes Islamic State in Iraq and Levant on its English website, but Islamischer Staat im Irak und Syrien (Islamic State in Iraq and Syria) on its German one. Other German publications like *Der Spiegel*, *Die Zeit* and the *Frankfurter Allgemeine* have chosen the acronym ISIS, and yet *Die Welt* prefers ISIL.[24]

To some security experts like Marc Peirini[25] (Visiting Scholar, Carnegie Europe) no purpose is served in settling 'mundane controversies' over the name of this group, while for others like French Foreign Minister Laurent Fabius the name is important as it reflects aspirations that the US and its allies unequivocally reject.[26]

5. The Genesis of the ISIS

The origins of the terror group ISIS can be traced back to the founding of Jamat-al-Tawheed-wal-Jihad (JTJ), translated as the 'Organization of Monotheism and Jihad,' by the notorious Iraqi militant Abu Musab Al-Zarqawi in 1999.

Al-Zarqawi had established contacts with Bin Laden while he was commanding his own group of fighters in Herat, Afghanistan, in the late 1990s.[27] Then in 2001, he moved to northern Iraq and joined *Ansar Al-Islam* and formed a group (JTJ) of militants who had fought in Afghanistan, Bosnia, Chechnya and Kashmir[28] with the aim of deposing the Jordanian monarchy. However, after the US-led invasion of

THE CRUCIBLE

CAMP BUCCA

The southern town of Garma in Iraq has been home to a sprawling detention center in Iraq called Camp Bucca, which is known as the early hotbed of ISIS extremism. Many ISIS leaders, including Abu Bakr al-Baghdadi, were once incarcerated in Camp Bucca and likely met there.

Former prison commander at the camp, James Skylar Gerrond remembers many inmates at the camp and says, "Many of us were concerned that instead of just holding detainees, we had created a pressure cooker for extremism." He worked at the prison between 2006 and 2007, when it was glutted with approximately 24,000 radicals, which reportedly included Baghdadi.

It is said that prisoners at Camp Bucca were divided along sectarian lines to ameliorate tension and that inmates settled their disputes by implementing Islamic law. It was in Camp Bucca that many former members of Saddam's Ba'athist military, like Haji Bakr, were radicalized and became members of the ISIS.

Iraq, JTJ focused primarily on fighting US-led coalition forces in Iraq. Here, the terrorist group was not only involved in carrying out attacks on US-led coalition forces but also conducted suicide attacks on civilian targets and the beheading of hostages.

Then on October 17, 2004, Al-Zarqawi and the JTJ organization issued an online statement pledging allegiance to Al-Qaeda and its leader, Osama bin Laden.[29] Al-Zarqawi also changed the name of his organization to Tanzim Qaidat al-Jihad fi Bilad al-Rifidadayn (The 'Organization of Jihad's Base in the Country of the Two Rivers'), but from here on was more commonly known as Al-Qaeda in Iraq (AQI).

After swearing 'bayah' (pledge of allegiance) to Osama bin Laden, the group launched major attacks on US-led coalition and emerged as the largest armed group in Iraq. Soon, the AQI became successful in clearing out US and Iraqi forces of some critical Sunni regions, beginning with Al-Anbar province.[30]

However, tensions reportedly grew between Al-Qaeda central and AQI, as the latter was seen as acting more independently and was accused of indulging in gruesome acts of violence that even Bin Laden did not approve of, for example the 2005 bombings by AQI of three hotels in Amman[31]. Although the AQI succeeded in gaining territories in Iraq's Sunni regions from the US and Iraqi forces, it also faced criticism from local tribes of being more foreign in its composition and for having fewer Iraqi members in its leadership.

In order to address these grievances, AQI decided to assemble smaller Iraqi insurgent groups under an umbrella organization called the Mujahideen Shura Council (MSC) in January 2006.[32] After the formation of the Council, the AQI became the dominant group in Azamiyah, Kazimiyah and Abu Ghraib neighborhoods of Baghdad.[33]

After Al-Zarqawi's death in a US airstrike on June 7, 2006, the leadership of the group passed on to Abu Ayyub Al Masri, also known as Abu Hamza Al Muhajir.

On October 12, 2006, the MSC brought the Soldiers of the Prophet's Companions (Jund Al-Sahaba), the Army of Conquerors (Jaish Al-Fatiheen) and the Army of the Victorious Sect (Jaish Al-Taif Al-Mansura) led by Umar Al Ansari into its fold by swearing the traditional Arab oath

'THE GODFATHER'

Abu Musab Al-Zarqawi (1966-2006)

Born as Ahmad Fadeel Al-Nazzal Al-Khalayleh in Zarqa (Jordan), Al-Zarqawi was founder of Al-Qaeda in Iraq (AQI) and responsible for series of bombings and beheadings during the Iraq War (i.e. from 2003 to 2006).

Over time, Bin Laden and Al-Zawahiri became critical of Al-Zarqawi's indiscriminate and sectarian violence, which they thought was proving counter-productive.

The rift widened after Al-Zarqawi died in a US air assault in 2006, leading to Al-Qaeda's eventual split with the AQI/ISI, rebranded as the ISIS in 2014. Al-Zarqawi, who is eulogised in ISIS literature, was killed when a US Air Force F-16 C jet dropped two 500-pound (230kg) guided bombs on his safehouse.

of allegiance – Hilf Al-Mutayyabin (Oath of the Scented Ones).[34] Following these mergers, the Council rebranded the AQI by declaring the establishment of the Islamic State of Iraq (ISI) on June 8, 2006. Abu Omar Al-Baghdadi was announced the Amir of this self-proclaimed state, while Al-Masri accepted the title of Minister of War in a 10-member cabinet.[35]

At its height, the ISI wielded substantial influence in Sunni-dominated areas of Al-Anbar, Nineveh, Kirkuk, parts of Babil and Salah ad Din, and even in parts of Baghdad. However, the declaration of the formation of an Islamic State at that time was criticized by many rival jihadist organizations in Iraq and several other jihadist ideologues.

The US viewed the formation of the Islamic State of Iraq with alarm and had warned at that time that such a state "will be a catastrophe and an imminent danger to Saudi Arabia and Jordan".[36] By May 2007, the ISI had come up with a draft constitution entitled "Notifying Mankind of the Birth of the Islamic State"[37] and was posted on a website based in Britain.

However, the birth of a coherent and contiguous Islamic State in Iraq's Sunni heartland was aborted by a new US strategy under General David Petraeus, who was appointed the Commander-in-Chief of Central Command (CENTCOM).

As part of the new Bush Doctrine, US deployed more troops in Iraq (known as the Iraq War Troop Surge of 2007) and formed the "Councils for the Awakening of Iraq" (given the name 'Sahwa' in Arabic) to convince Sunni tribes and insurgent groups to rise up against the ISI.[38]

The new US policy worked and played a key role in dramatically reducing violence across Iraq. During 2008, a series of US and Iraqi offensives managed to flush out AQI from its strongholds in Diyala and Al-Anbar governorates, as well as from areas around Baghdad to the city of Mosul.

By 2008, ISI admitted to being in a state of "extraordinary crisis".[39] It was at this time that the ISI started increasing the influence of Iraqi citizens in its ranks and reducing the clout of foreign fighters. Thus, it became customary for fighters to take on names that ended with names of Iraqi cities, such as Baghdadi, Samarrai etc.

However, the group faced another major blow when their two top leaders, Abu Ayyub Al-Masri and Abu Omar Al-Baghdadi were killed on 18 April 2010.[40]

The Ba'athist Behind Baghdadi

Haji Bakr

Samir Abd Muhammad Al-Khilfawi (died January 2014) is better known by the nom de guerre Haji Bakr was former colonel in Saddam's intelligence services and became the 'strategic head' of the ISIS.

Papers found in his house confirm earlier speculation that he and fellow intelligence officers were the actual leaders behind Al-Baghdadi. This indicates that the ISIS is essentially a Ba'athist-Al-Qaeda combine, exacting revenge on US-led coalition for the invasion of Iraq and for overthrowing historical Sunni dominance of Mesopotamia.

Haji Bakr was close associate of Baghdadi in Camp Bucca and it was at his instance that the Majlis Shura of the ISI inducted Baghdadi (a virtual unknown until then) into the Council and eventually made him the leader of the then ISI. Nearly a third of Baghdadi's top commanders are said to be former Baathists.

Then in June 2010, commander of the US forces in Iraq, General Ray Odierno reported that 80 percent of the ISI's top 42 leaders had been either killed or captured, and that only eight remained at large.[41] As part of efforts to replenish its forces and set the pace for reconstruction, ISI then took the important step of declaring amnesty to former Baathists.[42]

It is to be noted that the newly constituted Iraqi army did not recruit former Baathist soldiers. These trained soldiers now began to join the ranks of the ISI on the condition that "they showed repentance"[43] for being members of a former apostate army.

In fact, many of these experienced military personnel were assigned high level posts. One of these prominent former Baathist military officials was General Haji Bakr (Samir Al-Khilfawi),[44] who helped ISI launch its reconstruction campaign.

He developed new, more effective tactics for the group and found new connections and financial sources. Eventually, he was inducted in the elite Majlis Shura of the ISI. After the assassinations of Omar Al-Baghdadi and Al-Masri, the clout of Gen. Haji Bakr and his supporters increased in the Shura. It was at this time that Gen. Haji Bakr first proposed the name of a relatively unknown member of the ISI by the name of Abu Bakr Al-Baghdadi for inclusion to Majlis Al-Shura.

For its part, the central leadership of Al-Qaeda asked the ISI Shura for a report on Abu Bakr Al-Baghdadi's past, and whether he was a reliable and experienced person. It is noteworthy that until that time Abu Bakr Al-Baghdadi did not hold any significant position in the ISI. In its reply, the Shura stated that Al-Baghdadi was a person of merit, but Al-Qaeda leadership had the right to remove him if it deemed it appropriate. However, Al-Qaeda approved his inclusion in the Shura in order not to appear highly intrusive in the affairs of local bodies.[45]

Thus, within a month of the deaths of Omar Al-Baghdadi and Al-Masri, Abu Bakr Al-Baghdadi was appointed the new leader of the ISI (16 May, 2010).[46] Baghdadi expedited the process of induction of former Baathist military and intelligence officers into the ISI, most of whom had spent time with him in prisons of the US military (mainly in Camp Bucca).

It must be noted that nearly a third of Baghdadi's top military commanders are former Baathists. The year 2011 saw the renewal of the

ISI threat. As the process of the US troop withdrawal from Iraq began, ISI carried out bomb attacks and targeted Iraqi and coalition security forces, as well as leaders of the Sunni Awakening (Sahwa) Councils.

In the wake of the Arab Spring, Syria was getting destabilized and a civil war loomed in that country. Sensing opportunity to spread the ISI menace, Al-Baghdadi sent his foreign fighters, particularly Syrians to enter that country and form their insurgent group there. "ISI had contacted Al-Qaeda Center for this and been given permission to form a branch in Syria on condition of keeping Al-Qaeda nom de guerres and connections in secret."[47]

Thus, on 23 January 2012, the group Jabhat Al-Nusra li Ahl-As Sham - translated as the Front of Victory in Al-Sham region and commonly known as Jabhat Al-Nusrah (JN) or the Nusrah Front -

&

Baghdadi expedited the process of induction of former Baathist military and intelligence officers into the ISI, most of whom had spent time with him in prisons of the US military (mainly Camp Bucca). It must be noted that nearly a third of Baghdadi's top military commanders are former Baathists.

&

came into existence, under the leadership of Abu Muhammad Al-Jawlani. It soon became a highly capable fighting force and gained a lot of support from Syrian people opposed to the regime of Bashar Al-Assad.[48]

The success of JN, with its growing popularity among Syrians, huge financial support from Sunni donors in the region, large cache of weaponry and munitions seized from Assad's military, created a rift between Al-Baghdadi and his protégé Al-Jawlani in Syria.

In fact, ISI asked Al-Jawlani to disband JN and announce his commitment to ISI. When Al-Jawlani refused, Haji Bakr reached Syria and tried to take over the reins of JN as well as called on its leadership to pledge obedience to Al-Baghdadi, but to no avail.

Evolution of ISIS Since 1999

Earlier Incarnations	Period	Leaders
Jama'at Al Tawheed wal Jihad (JTJ)	Late 1999 - 17 Oct. 2004	Abu Mus'ab Al-Zarqawi
Al-Qaeda fi Bilad Al Rafiday (Al-Qaeda in Iraq, AQI)	17 Oct. 2004-15 Jan. 2006	Abu Mus'ab Al-Zarqawi Abu Omar Al-Baghdadi
Majlis Al Shura Al Mujahideen (MSM)	15 Jan. - 15Oct. 2006	Abu Ayyub Al-Masri
Islamic State of Iraq (ISI)	15 Oct. 2006-9 April 2013	Abu Ayyub Al-Masri Abu Bakr Al-Baghdadi (since May 2010)
Islamic State of Iraq and Al-Shaam (ISIS)	9 April 2013-29 June 2014	Abu Bakr Al-Baghdadi
The So-Called Islamic State	29 June 2014-present	Abu Bakr Al-Baghdadi Abu Alaa Al-Afri (Officiating) Since March 2015

Then in April 2013, Al-Baghdadi issued an audio statement that the ISI and the JN were merging into a new group, which he called the Islamic State of Iraq and Al-Sham (ISIS).

In response, Al-Jawlani complained that "neither the Al-Nusrah command nor its consultative authority, nor its general manager were aware of this announcement. It reached them via the media and if the speech is authentic we were not consulted."[49] He added that JN will not be changing its flag or its "behavior".

To settle this dispute between the feuding Jihadist organizations, the new Al-Qaeda leader Ayman Al-Zawahari stepped in to the fray in June 2013 and issued a ruling[50] that instructed ISIS to focus its activities solely in Iraq, even as JN concentrates its activities in Syria. Al-Qaeda high command also ordered both affiliates to support each other and appointed Abu Musab Al-Suri (founder of another Al-Qaeda group called Ahrar Al-Sham) as the judge of any future disagreements between the two.

Although the decision was accepted by JN, Abu Bakr Al-Baghdadi soon released an audio message in which he rejected Al-Zawahiri's ruling and declared that he will not accept the separation of the two groups' areas of activities based on borders carved out as per the Sykes-Picot agreement. Thereafter, ISIS took control of JN's military and financial sources and sought allegiance of new groups of foreign fighters entering Syria.[51] Some jihadist groups that were not admitted by JN, such as Jaish Al Muhajireen wal Ansar and a young Chechen group led by Omar Al-Shishani joined the ISIS ranks. Again, several foreign fighters left JN forces and joined the ISIS. The dispute between the two jihadist groups took an uglier turn when ISIS refused the trial of its men in JN's Sharia court, announcing that they will be judged only in an ISIS court.

> In October 2013, Al-Qaeda Supremo Ayman Al-Zawahari issued an explicit order: "ISIS is not a branch of the Qaidat al-Jihad (Al-Qaeda's official name) group, we have no organizational relationship with it, and the group is not responsible for its actions."

Then in October 2013, Al-Zawahari issued an explicit order for the disbanding of the ISIS and making JN solely in charge of Al-Qaeda's war effort in Syria. When the rebellious Baghdadi failed to conform to the ruling and ISIS continued to wage war in Syria on its own, then Al-Qaeda finally disavowed any relation with ISIS on February 2014. The Al-Qaeda statement to this effect read: "ISIS is not a branch of the Qaidat al-Jihad (Al-Qaeda's official name) group, we have no organizational relationship with it, and the group is not responsible for its actions."[52]

Since then, the hatred became so intense that the two sides started killing one another in battle, which even led to the death of Al-Qaeda emissary Abu Khalid Al-Suri in a suspected ISIS suicide attack.[53]

Relations between Al-Qaeda and ISIS hit an all-time low in June

2014, when after sweeping through vast swaths of Iraq's Sunni-dominated regions, Abu Bakr Al-Baghdadi proclaimed himself the 'Khalifah' (Caliph) of the global Muslim community and asked all Muslims to pledge their allegiance to him.[54] This audacity of Al-Baghdadi upset Al-Zawahiri who denounced the declaration. Most rival Jihadist organizations and many extremist ideologues like Abu Qatada al-Filistini, Iyad Qunaybi, Hani Al-Sibai, Yusuf Al-Qaradawi and Al-Maqdisi joined Al-Qaeda in disavowing ISIS. However, recent US bombardment in ISIS-held territories in Syria and Iraq has brought the two sides somewhat closer and there has been reduction in violence against each other, along with attempts at a rapprochement.

The Spring of 2015 has dealt new setbacks to the ISIS. The group lost control of the strategic city of Tikrit, Saddam's birthplace and Sunni stronghold, in a pitched battle with Iraqi military forces. The 72-year-old Saddam loyalist and ISIS-supporter Izzat Ibrahim Al-Dourri was reportedly killed in the battle. The other blow was the news of Abu Bakr Al-Baghadi's apparent incapacitation (the report of his death by Iran Radio's remains unconfirmed) due to severe spinal injury in a US airstrike on March 18, 2015. The organization was then said to be led by Al-Baghdadi's deputy, Abu Ala'a Al-Afri. However, there are unconfirmed reports of him being killed in one of the US airstrikes as well.[55]

In spite of these setbacks, the ISIS managed to wrest control of the strategic city of Ramadi from the Iraqi forces by May 2015 and were said to be slowly converging to the country's biggest oil refinery in Baiji.[56] They are also said to have taken control of the historic city of Palmyra[57] and the threat of the desecration and loot of this historical site, similar to the ISIS' earlier bulldozing of the ancient cities of Nimrud and Hatra, has raised international concern.

Chapter Two
Ideology: Quest for the Caliphate

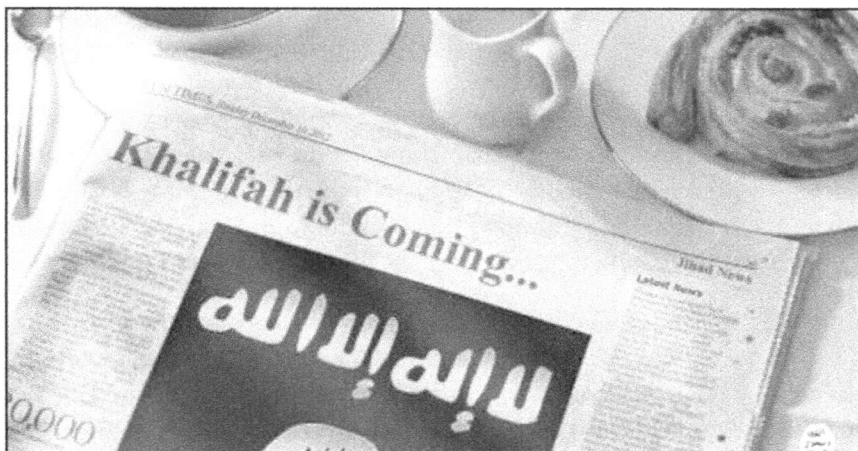

Picture of ISIS online propaganda to garner support for the rise of the
Caliphate

*"The goal of establishing the Khilafah (Caliphate) has always been one that
occupied the hearts of the Mujahideen (Muslim fighters) since the revival of
jihad this century."*

ISIS online magazine *Dabiq*, Issue 1,
(Page 33, Chapter 'From Hijrah to Khilafah')

6.   Islam Versus 'Islamism'

While delivering a lecture at the Hebrew University of Jerusalem,
internationally acclaimed Islamic historian Bernard Lewis pointed out
that "Mohammed, unlike the founders of other religions, triumphed
during his lifetime. Moses did not reach the Promised Land, Jesus was
crucified. Mohammed did not suffer either of these disagreeable things. He

conquered the Promised Land and became its ruler."[58]

Ironically, it is this fact which has brought both exaltation and confusion to Islamic religious scholarship down the ages. To most orthodox scholars of Sunni Islam, the formation of the Prophet's state in Arabia was a natural but incidental corollary to his divinely inspired religious and spiritual mission. However, to the many proponents of political Islam or 'Islamism' of the 19th and 20th century, the Prophetic mission's ascendance to political and state power was fundamental to and the logical culmination of the divinely ordained cause. Thus for Islamists, the attainment of political power often through militant struggle gains primacy over other spiritual, intellectual and ethical endeavors in religion and remains the principal means for reinstating Islam to its pristine glory. Not surprisingly, one of the earliest Islamist organizations, Muslim Brotherhood of Egypt has been known to preach the maxim *"al-islam deenun wa dawlatun"* (Islam is a religion and a state), even though this idea does not find a parallel in the Quran and Hadeeth literature.[59]

Thus to properly comprehend the ISIS ideology and its worldview, it will be important to first understand its ideological roots that lie in the rise of modern political Islam, which is also known as 'Islamism'. Distinct from the orthodox Islamic tradition, Islamism is a revisionist political and ideological movement which attempts at reinterpreting the Quran and Hadeeth literature, often as a counterpoint and an antithesis to modern Western political systems and social values. Its raison d'etre is to reverse the decline of Muslim political power, which once dominated the world but started to decline around the 17th century, with the rise of European colonialism. Thus, Islamism has been defined by Fred Halliday as "the organised political trend, owing its modern origin to the founding of the Muslim Brotherhood in Egypt in 1928, which seeks to solve modern political problems by reference to Muslim texts"[60].

In fact, many of the tenets of Islamism were developed in the 20th century by Muslim intellectuals and activists like Abul Ala Maududi (1903-79), Hassan Al Banna (1906-49), Syed Qutb (1906-66), Allama Iqbal (1877-1938), Taqiuddin Al-Nabhani (1909-77), Abdullah Azzam (1941-89) and others. Most of these Islamists called for the establishment of a non-monarchical, collectivist, theocratic state for the eventual realization of a utopian Islamic order. However, most Islamists have differing interpretations of Islamic law and support an outlook which is skeptical toward individual liberty and free enquiry. In the words of Daniel Pipes, Islamism is a modern ideology that owes more to European political ideologies and "isms" than to the traditional Islamic religion.[61]

Although many Islamic political activists oppose the use of the term 'Islamism' by claiming their goals and beliefs are simply an expression of Islamic religious beliefs, non-Islamist scholars of Islam often complain that many Western governments at times fail to distinguish between Islam and Islamism to the detriment of the apolitical and moderate practitioners of faith, who seek to separate the religion of Islam from politics and extremism.[62]

It is important to note here that this study focuses on the study of Sunni 'Islamism', as much as it relates to the evolution of the ISIS ideology and that the Shiite political revivalist movements lie outside its scope.

Thus, it is important to note that many Sunni jihadist organizations of our times have risen from modern Islamic religious reform movements like Wahhabism, Salafism etc. These groups rose in opposition to not only the growing Western influences in the 19th century but curiously reinterpreted religion based on the principles of extreme rationality and literalism, which was very modern in approach and at variance with the orthodox juristic schools. Thus, the ideology and doctrines that guide the so-called fundamentalist and zealous extremist groups in Islam today belong more to the reformist schools that arose to correct the so-called 'corruption' in Islamic practices by the end of 18th and 19th centuries.

Most members of the ISIS avowedly follow the Salafi school of Sunni Islam and a terrorist

ℰᗧᏣᏅ

Sunni Islamists claim that since the time the Turkish Caliphate was dissolved in 1924, the Muslim world has been riddled with conflicts and disintegration. They view Western political, military, economic and cultural expansion in modern times as a form of aggression, which they believe obligates every Muslim to fight in order to expel the West from Islamic lands and reestablish the Caliphate

ℰᗧᏣᏅ

and millenarian orientation with a vision of creating a Sunni Islamic Caliphate by merging all Muslim states into its version of Sharia (Islamic law)-based political empire under the leadership of a 'Khalifah' (Caliph in English language, literally the 'successor' of Prophet Muhammad). It seeks to find its primacy in Islamic eschatological prophecies, mentioned in Ahadeeth (sayings of the Prophet), to claim its future historic role and significance. The group seeks to violently cleanse people of other religious communities, as well as many Shiite and Sufi sects as part of its doctrine of 'takfeer' (declaring people apostate and thereby liable for slaughter).

Many of the tenets of ISIS ideology are derived from concepts developed in the 20th century by exponents of Islamism, even though most Islamists do not espouse violence as a means to attain their Islamist objectives. The principal exponents of Islamism in the 20th century were Abul Ala Maududi, Hassan Al Banna, Syed Qutb and Abdullah Azzam. However, Islamists are not necessarily Jihadists

In the words of Ayeman Al Tamimi, Distinguished Senior Fellow of the Gatestone

Forerunner of Salafi Jihadism

Ibn Taimiyyah

Taqi Ad-din Ahmad Ibn Taimiyyah (22 January 1263 – 26 September 1328) is a controversial Islamic theologian and logician. He lived through the difficult times of Mongol invasion of the Abbasid empire.

He is known for issuing the fatwa of 'takfeer' (apostasy) against 'barbaric' Mongol kings, declaring jihad by Muslims against them as compulsory, in spite of their conversion to Islam. He also called on Sunnis to return to ways of the 'Salaf', (the Prophet's companions) and is in this way a forerunner of Salafism. These ideas profoundly influenced the Wahhabi and Salafi movements, as well as Jihadism in modern times.

Institute and a Shillman/Ginsburg Writing Fellow at the Middle East Forum: "The answer formulated by ideologues of the global jihad movement is that the cause of this decline (the regression of Muslim power in modern times) is the result of the Muslim world's deviation from the path of Islam and its inability to impose Islamic law in the social and political spheres." This, they claim, stands in contrast to the time of the 'Islamic Golden Age' in the first five centuries of Islam, "when the Muslim world was supposedly uncontaminated by foreign influences."[63] Although the Islamist portrayal of this era is blatantly unhistorical, still it is the perception that matters.

Although opposed to the hereditary monarchical order prevalent to this day in the Islamic world, Islamism is equally antithetical to modern political systems as well (e.g. democracy, communism, fascism and nationalism). It calls for reverting to the pre-feudal, puritanical political order established by the four Pious Caliphs (the first four Caliphs of Islam) who ruled the pristine Islamic state. According to Abul Ala Maududi, founder of Jamaat-i-Islami movement in the Indian subcontinent who left a deep influence on Qutb, argued that Islam is not merely a religion; it is a "revolutionary ideology and program which seeks to alter the social order of the whole world."[64]

For Islamists, all Muslims of the world constitute a single nation and they should eventually become politically united under a Caliphate to safeguard their religious and territorial interests. Sunni Islamists claim that since the time the Turkish Caliphate (although viewed as corrupt in itself) was dissolved in 1924, the Muslim world has been riddled with war, conflict and disintegration. In this context, they view Western political, military, economic and cultural expansion in modern times as a form of aggression, which some of its extreme exponents like Abdullah Azzam aver obligates every Muslim "to expel the Kuffar (infidels) from our land"[65] and reestablish the Caliphate. This ideological aspiration is common to various Sunni non-violent as well as militant organizations, particularly Al-Qaeda and its affiliates, like the ISIS. However, it is in the Salafi-Wahhabi school of Sunni Islam that the message of modern Jihadism has found a fertile soil.

Although Salafis constitute only 3 percent of the world's Muslim population, and the overwhelming majority of Salafi Muslims are considered to be strictly apolitical and non-violent (particularly the Madkhali Salafis),[66] the fact that the sect does not align itself to any classical Islamic school of jurisprudence and seeks a reversion to the pristine practices of the 'Salaf' (the early generation of pious Muslims) draws the 'modern' proponents of revisionist, pan-Islamism close to adherents of this school of Sunni Islam.

In fact, both Wahhabism and Salafism that arose in the 18th century and 19th centuries were reactionary religious-political movements, which revolted against the classical schools of Islamic scholasticism. Therefore, their adherents find 20th century Islamist preoccupation of reformulating Islam, free of its medieval cultural trappings and based solely on a rationalist, fundamentalist reinterpretation of early Islam as highly appealing.

In the words of Nuh Keller,[67] "With the neatness of mind which they (the Salafis) had learnt from the West, and driven by a giddy enthusiasm which blinded them to the finer aspects of the classical heritage, many of the fundamentalists announced that they found the Islam of the people horribly untidy. Why not sweep away all the medieval cobwebs, and create a bright new Islam, streamlined and ready to take its place as an ideology alongside Marxism, capitalism, and secular nationalism? To achieve this aim, it was thought that the four *madhhabs* of *fiqh* had to go. Ditto for the Ash`ari and Maturidi theological traditions. The Sufi orders were often spectacularly exotic and untidy: they of course had to be expunged as well. In fact, at least ninety percent of the traditional Islamic texts could happily be consigned to the shredding machine: while what was left, it was hoped, would be the Islam of the Prophet, stripped of unsightly barnacles, and presiding over a reunified Muslim world, striding towards a new and shining destiny."

7. The Decline of Secular Pan-Arabism

The rise of Islamism in the Muslim world toward the latter half of the 20th century, can be seen as a reaction to secular, pan-Arab nationalist movements that swept across the Muslim world in the wake of the two World Wars. With the dismemberment of the dynastic Ottoman Caliphate after World War I, West Asia was carved up into British and French Mandates under the secretive Sykes Picot Agreement. Allied powers drew straight lines on the West Asian map to create new nation states.

Former Ottoman governors and Arab allies of the Great War were installed as puppet rulers in these fledgling realms. However, a rising tide of Arab nationalism soon overthrew many of these rulers around the end of World War II and new totalitarian regimes emerged, such as in Egypt (under Gemal Abdel Nasser), in Iraq and Syria (under the rule of Ba'ath parties), in Algeria and Libya (under Ahmed Ben Bellah and Muammar Gaddafi) and in the Arabian Peninsula (under ruling families like the House of Saud). This so-called period of 'Arab renaissance' was short-lived though, as the defeat of Arab states in the 'Six Day War' of 1967 against Israel shattered the ideal of pan-Arabism and drew an ever widening wedge between Arab masses and their leaderships. As discontent grew, most Arab regimes adopted repressive policies to remain in power.

Meanwhile, the West's unstinted support for Israel (frequently championed as the model of democracy and modernization in the region) turned popular Arab sentiments against the West as well as towards its avowed principles of liberalism and democracy. In fact, prior to the outbreak of the so-called 'Arab Spring' in 2011, Western powers and international organizations hardly supported liberal political movements in the Arab world, even when such popular uprisings were brutally crushed by despotic regimes.

It is in this environment that the groundswell of opposition grew more radical, anti-Western and increasingly veered towards religious extremism. Even the somewhat moderate and democratic Islamist parties, like the Muslim Brotherhood of Egypt, were radicalized and became the breeding ground for extremist thinkers like Sayyid Qutb (1906-66) and Abdullah Azzam (1941-89). As the largely secular, socialist regimes turned

---

Muhammad ibn Abdel Al-Wahhab (1703-92)

He was a preacher and scholar from Nejd in central Arabia, who started a movement to purify Islam by returning Muslims to what he believed were the original principles of the faith. The movement started by him is called 'Wahhabism', although its adherents regard this term as derogatory and one coined by its opponents. They call themselves Salafis, although they differ from mainstream Salafis in subtle ways, particularly on matters of kingship.

In his book *Kitab Al-Tawheed*, Abd Al Wahhab states that calling upon the help or intercession from anyone or anything other than God in prayer contradicts the Islamic tenets of Tawheed (the Oneness of God). Therefore, he called Muslims who committed such acts as apostates. He helped establish the first Saudi state and began a dynastic and power-sharing agreement with the family.

totalitarian, Islamist movements raised the banner of popular revolt and reasoned that the Arab world needed moral and religious revival to eliminate the "socio-political contamination" festered by Western values.

Thus, the unifying slogan of secular, pan-Arab renaissance was replaced with hard-core Islamic resurgence. Even the concept of jihad was redefined by ideologues like Sayyid Qutb and Muhammad Abd-al-Salam Farag. The traditional understanding of the Islamic principle of Jihad (struggle) in its military sense was a war of defense against non-believers.[68] However, Sayyid Qutb argued that not only was Jihad an offensive war, but it could also be waged against internal enemies — including the state, if it had lost its legitimacy.

Traditional Islamic legal thought had always given precedence to stability and order over political legitimacy and had expressed strong disapproval of rebellions and armed opposition to state authority. However, in his book Maʿalim fiʾl-tareeq (translated as Milestones), Qutb writes: "If we insist on calling Islamic jihad a defensive movement, then we must change the meaning of the word 'defense' — and mean by it 'the defense of man' against all those forces that limit his freedom."[6]

It is often said that without the writings of Qutb "Al-Qaeda would not have existed."[70] It was Qutb who believed that in the absence of Shariah law, the Muslim world was no longer Muslim but had declined to pre-Islamic ignorance known as 'jahiliyya'. He believed "rightful Muslims" should seek to establish "truly Islamic states" to rid the Muslim world of non-Islamic influences of socialism and nationalism.

Qutb also believed that many Muslims, who claimed to be the true followers of Islam, were actually apostates.[71] Such Muslims included rulers of Islamic countries, who should be removed from power and executed as they failed to establish Islamic law in their countries. He reinterpreted the Islamic term 'jahiliyyah' (ignorance of divine guidance) as the domination of humans over humans, rather than submission of humans to God.

Qutb also warned the Muslim world against "treacherous Orientalists" and "world Jewry", which wickedly plotted against Islam.[72] Among the ardent followers of Qutb in Al-Qaeda were some of its top leaders, namely Mafouz Azzam and Ayman Al Zawahari.

THE INDIAN ISLAMIST

Abul Ala Maududi
(1903-79)

One of the most influential Muslim scholars of the 20th century, he was the founder of the largest Islamic organization in Asia, Jamaat-e-Islami.

Maududi believed that politics was an essential component of Islam and necessary to institute 'Shariah' (Islamic law) as well as to preserve Islamic culture from the evils of nationalism, modernism and secularism.

He believed that Quran was not merely meant for spiritual enlightenment, but was a guide for socio-political transformation.

Taking the concept of Jihad a step further were radical ideologues like Muhammad Abd-al-Salam Farag (1954-82), who argued that the Arab/Muslim world has been in a state of decline ever since the Caliphate was annulled after World War I.

Thus, the purpose of Jihad, they claimed, should be to enable Muslims reestablish the Caliphate (a single Islamic state based on Shariah and comprising all Muslims under a 'Khalifah') and then to rule the world. It is for this reason that Islamists are opposed to the ideal of nationalism and nation-states, as nations are carved on the basis of ethnic or territorial identity and not the identity of belief (Iman), which Islamists believe is the true basis for personal identity. In his book titled *The Neglected Duty*,[73] Farag approves of even illegitimate forms of traditional Jihad, such as deceiving the enemy, lying to him, attacking by night (even of it leads to accidentally killing innocents), and felling and burning trees of the infidel. Farag was eventually executed in 1982 after he was found guilty of coordinating the assassination of Egyptian president Anwar Sadat.

8.   Ascendance of Wahhabi and Salafi Movements

The appeal of political Islam grew at the expense of pan-Arabism as it equated the decline in Arab power with the degeneration of its religious/spiritual strength, which it claimed was the result of Arab adherence to corrupt Western values and lifestyle and the abandonment of Islamic traditions. It criticized pan-Arabism for having a racist and secularist orientation, which extolled a common culture and language, while remaining unmindful of its spiritual and religious underpinnings. This idea gained particular traction among the so-called reformist religious movements, particularly the Salafi and Wahhabi ideology of Sunni Islam, to which terrorist organizations Al-Qaeda and ISIS belong.

Both Wahhabi and Salafi schools of Sunni Islam emerged as revivalist movements in the 18th and 19th centuries respectively. However, over the decades the two have been described so differently and their names have been used so interchangeably that it has become very difficult to define them in a way that encapsulates the beliefs of all their adherents. Therefore, any definition runs the risk of being inaccurate to some degree.

Again, the concept of Salafi Islam has evolved to the extent that it has merged Wahhabism into its fold and today even the adherents of Muhammad Abdul Wahhab (founder of Wahhabism) call themselves Salafis, as they have always disliked the term 'Wahhabi,' which was initially used pejoratively by the detractors of the religious movement. In fact, Wahhabism is today viewed as a particular orientation within Salafism, or an ultra-conservative, Saudi version of Salafism.

The first Islamic scholar to have introduced concepts like reverting to the practices of the 'Salaf' (the first three generations from the time of the Prophet) and 'takfeer' (declaring people apostate to legitimize their killing) was the Syrian logician and theologian Taqi Ad-din Ahmad Ibn Taimiyyah (1263 –1328 AD). However, the movement we know as Wahhabism was founded by Muhammad ibn Abd al-Wahhab (1703-92), who was born in the Najd region of modern Saudi Arabia. A strict exponent of monotheism, Abd al-Wahhab claimed that the decline of the Muslim world was the result of gradual accretion of non-Islamic influences in Islamic faith and practices.

He believed that contemporary Islamic scholasticism had strayed from its origins and had become decadent. His stated mission was to revive Islam by following 'the Salaf' (literally 'ancestors', referring to the companions of the Prophet) in order to restore pristine Islam from the recent corruptions of 'shirk' (worship of other entities besides God, considered the worst sin), 'bida'h' (innovation), 'tawassul' (intercession of saints) and 'taqleed' (blindly following religious scholars).

Founder of 20th Century Jihadism

Sayyid Qutb (1906-66)

Egyptian Islamic theorist, poet and member of the Muslim Brotherhood, Qutb is known for his intense disapproval of the society and culture of the US and its "obsession with materialism and sexual pleasures". His writings are also highly critical of Muslim leaders whom he deemed as non-Islamic dictators and puppets of the West.

Qutb supported a non-dictatorial, non-democratic egalitarian Islamic order. He was executed for plotting assassination of the then Egyptian President Gemal Abdel Nasser in 1966. His ideas influenced Al-Qaeda.

He called on Muslims for strict adherence to the concept of 'tawheed' (belief in oneness of God as well as only His worship).[74] Thus, the Wahhabi/Salafi school of Islam calls for strict adherence of the belief that Allah is one, and that He does not share or delegate His power to anyone (Tawheed-e-Rubibyah), that He alone is worthy of worship in His transcendent glory (Tawheed-e-Ululiyah) and that He has special names and attributes mentioned in the Quran, which one should believe in (Tawheed-e-Asma wal Siffat).

According to Abd Al-Wahhab, any belief or practice which violates the understanding of Tawheed is an act of *shirk* (associating a created thing with Godhead), the only unpardonable sin in Islam, which makes even a Sunni Muslim an apostate.

Abd Al-Wahhab went a step further and targeted the religious practices of the Sunni Sufis and the Shiites. He alleged they had accorded holy status to their saints and promoted the worship of their graves, in the name of their intercession to God on behalf of the plaintiff.

Many non-Salafist Sunni Muslims allege that the above categorization of Tawheed by Salafists is their own invention and that this was first introduced by Ibn Taymiyyah. Ibn Taymiyyah and Abdel Wahhab were also strictly opposed to the Sufi concept of 'Wahdatul Wajud' (the Oneness of God and Creation). They call it a monistic concept, which they contend leads to pantheism and idolatry.

In fact, they strictly advocated declaring Muslims having such beliefs as apostates or 'Mushrikeen' (those who include multiple entities to Godhead).

In his book *Kitab Al Tawheed*, Abd Al-Wahhab states that Christians and Jews were also apostates, as they indulged in sorcery and devil worship. The Muslim detractors of Abd Al-Wahhab maintain that Islam accords a special status to Christians and Jews by calling them *Ahl-e-Kitab* (People of the Book), in recognition of the fact that they received the divine revelations of God in the form of Torah and the Gospel.[75] They also point out that Islam does not sanction violence and negation of human rights of non-Muslims.

It is important to note that Muhammad ibn Abd Al Wahhab was instrumental in establishing the first Saudi state, known as the emirate of Diriyah, in 1744. In fact, he instituted a dynastic alliance and power sharing agreement with the Saud family, which some Salafi scholars view as an unacceptable act that has legitimized hereditary despotism since then.

Problems within Wahhabism began in the early 20th century, when much of the Arabia united under the leadership of Al-Saud family. The main tool for achieving this unification was the 'Ikhwan', a Wahhabi-Bedoiun tribal army that after the collapse of the Ottoman Caliphate and the help of Britain after World War1, established Abdul Aziz I as the King of the Hejaz and the King of Nejad in 1927, thus forming the kingdom of Saudi Arabia.

However, after the conquest of the Hejaz, some Ikhwan leaders wished to continue expanding the Wahhabist realm into the British protectorates of Iraq, Transjordan and Kuwait. Abdul Aziz Al-Saud, however, refused to agree with his Ikhwan supporters in this matter. Although the Ikhwan had been taught that all non-Wahabbis were infidels, Abdul-Aziz was aware that these new areas of central Arabia had treaties with London. As he himself had just won British recognition as an independent ruler and recognized the danger of a direct conflict with the British, he opposed destabilizing other Muslim regimes in the neighborhood.

For their part, the Ikhwan became deeply critical of the Saudi King's position and openly revolted against him on December 1928. Although, this revolt was crushed in the Battle of Sabilla in March 1929, the animosity between the remnants of the Ikhwan and the Saud family continued.[76] The present members of Al-Qaeda and the ISIS, have an ideological affinity with the Ikhwan rebels and continue to carry on the fight against the Saudi rulers till date, as they charge the Saudi family for being despotic and hypocritical towards its averred religious convictions.

As for Salafism, the movement began in a different place and time from the Wahhabi movement, in spite of its current ideological affinities with Wahhabism. The Salafi sect of Sunni Islam originated in Egypt and developed in the mid-19th century, almost a century after the birth of Wahhabism. It began as a religious reform movement, spearheaded by religious scholars like Muhammad Abduh (1849-1905), Jamal Al Din Afghani (1839-97) and Rashid Rida (1865-1935). In fact the term Salafism was first used by Rashid Rida to describe the views of his mentor, Muhammad Abduh.

The early Salafis admired the technological and social advancement of the European enlightenment and sought the Muslim community to likewise revive the rational, intellectual and scientific advancements of the Golden Age of Islam that emerged after Prophet Muhammad's revelations.[77] It is important to note that Hassan Al-Banna was highly influenced by the early Salafi ideologues like Muhammad Abduh and Rashid Rida, which led him to establish the Muslim Brotherhood in Egypt in 1928.

Most of the views of these early Salafi Islamists, which sought to reconcile Islam with modernism, were almost completely abandoned by their future adherents.[78] In fact, later Salafis found the 'takfeeri' teachings of controversial medieval scholars like Ibn Taymiyyah more attractive. Being rationalists, they favored a literalist and fundamentalist "re-interpretation" of the religious texts, without resorting to the understanding of classical scholarship and often allegedly without seeking the proper context and syntax to appreciate the intended meaning. The sect gradually disaffiliated themselves from the four orthodox Sunni schools of thought (madhhabs), and in pursuit of a pristine form of Islam, seemingly practiced by the Salaf (the early Muslims and companions of the Prophet after whom the movement has been named), adopted a highly rigid and fundamentalist outlook that over the decades developed a close affinity with Wahhabism. Several historically controversial scholars like Ibn Taymiyyah, Abdel Aziz bin Baz, Muhammad ibn Al-Uthaymeen and Muhammad Nasiruddin Al-Albani gained precedence in Salafi Islam over several other historically established Sunni scholars.

The process of the ideological commingling between Salafi and Wahhabi schools of thought began in the period between 1920 and 1960, when Saudi Arabia was striving to become a modern state. With increased oil production and rising development, the administration needed qualified educators, bureaucrats and engineers from abroad, whose religious views and practices was not alien to that of its less educated populace. Muslim Brotherhood (then a hotbed of Salafism) became a natural source for such qualified professionals, who were also willing to come to Saudi Arabia to escape their repression in Egypt. As Nasser's pan-Islamism suffered a decline, King Faisal of Saudi Arabia sought to replace it with his Salafi-Wahhabi brand of pan-Islamism. In fact, Saudi Arabia founded and funded several Salafi organizations, which had their headquarters in the country. One of the most well-known of these establishments was the World Muslim Organization that was founded in Mecca in 1962.

Over a period of time, Salafi movement developed disparate strands (such as Madkhali, Suroori, Qutbi etc.) ranging from apolitical, non-violently political, anti-despotic to outright militant Jihadi groups fighting against the Saudi Kingdom itself. It is believed that only 10 percent of Salafis today belong to the Jihadist school of thought, with a large majority pursuing an apolitical and non-violent ideology. Salafis are the "dominant minority" in Saudi Arabia. They are also found in large numbers in the states of Qatar, UAE, Bahrain, Kuwait and Egypt.

One of the earliest, virulent forms of Salafiyya Jihadism was witnessed in 1979, when a group of young Salafi insurgents that called for the overthrow of the House of Saud and took control of the Kaaba (from November 20 to December 4, 1979) in the city of Mecca, during the annual Haj pilgrimage.

The insurgents - led by a charismatic 43 year old militant Juhayman Al Otaybi - claimed that one of their leaders was the mythical Mahdi himself (an end-time Muslim world conqueror in Islamic eschatology), a person by the name of Muhammad Abdullah Al-Qahtani. The siege ended after two weeks of much bloodshed and the execution of Otaybi and his cohorts. Since then the Saudi state has implemented a strict Islamic code to maintain order in the country.

But the threat posed by Salafiyya Jihadism, opposed to the despotic rule of the House of Saud, continues to trouble Saudi authorities, principally those associated with Osama bin Laden's Al-Qaeda, which includes the ISIS. Some critics of the Saudi government blame it for having fostered radical Jihadist ideologues only to suffer the consequences later.

It is pointed out that during the rule of King Khalid (who reigned from 1975-1982) important proponents of Qutbism, including Abdullah Azzam, Umar Abd Al-Rahman and Muhammad Qutb, served as educators in the kingdom. In fact, the brother of Sayyid Qutb is said to have played a major role in writing several texts on 'Tawheed' for the Saudi school curriculum.

9.   Al-Qaeda and the Justification of Terrorism

Taking cue from the ideological diktats of Maududi, Qutb and Azzam, Al-Qaeda (the overarching ideological and financial sponsor of Salafiyaa Jihadism) added terrorism as the mode of its "religiously inspired violence," for which it has been strongly criticized by classical Islamic scholarship over the years. As a true offshoot of Qaidat Al-Jihad (the name by which Al-Qaeda calls itself), the ISIS follows its teacher's justification for committing acts of terrorism in the name of Jihad and has taken it to levels which even Al-Qaeda finds gruesome.

It is noteworthy that the concept of jihad "as a war to increase the sphere of Islam" came in vogue only among later Islamic jurists[79]. Although Islam strictly forbids the killing of non-combatants in war, Al-Qaeda provided reasons for targeting civilian targets in its war against the West after it drew a lot of flak from Islamic scholars following the 9/11 terrorist attacks. On April 24, 2002, Al-Qaeda released an extended statement (approximately 3,700 words) outlining, for the first time, its religious justification for killing civilians in a total war against the United States, titled 'A Statement from Qaidat Al-Jihad Regarding the Mandates of the Heroes and the Legality of the Operations in New York and Washington.'"[80] In it, Al-Qaeda listed seven conditions which nullify Islamic prohibition against killing of civilians and using terrorism as a ploy to defeat the enemy.[81] These include

> ➢ The norm of reciprocity (when the aggressor, like the US or Israel in Palestine or Iraq, indulges in killing civilians, Al-Qaeda argues

the limitation of not killing civilians becomes invalid for the resistance)

➢ The inability to distinguish civilians from combatants as the theatre of war today is not restricted to traditional battlefields.

➢ The role of civilians in aiding the enemy and their responsibility in electing democratic representatives that launch wars against Muslim states.

➢ Transformation of enemy 'strongholds' that are no longer just military targets but economic centers, like the World Trade Center, which financially support the military.

➢ The use of modern weaponry which invariably entails collateral damage

➢ The acceptability of killing women and children if the enemy uses them as human shields (called *turs*)

➢ Enemy's violation of agreements or treaties (like the betrayal of the Sykes-Picot agreement and the creation of Israel) which puts lives of Muslim populations in danger, then the protection of enemy civilians is invalidated.

10.   Ideological Dissonance Within Al-Qaeda After 9/11 Attacks

The enormity of the crime committed by Al-Qaeda by using civilian passenger planes to attack the Twin Towers of the World Trade Center in New York and the Pentagon in the US on September 11 2001, killing thousands of civilians and creating shockwaves of horror and revulsion throughout the world, swiftly boomeranged on the organization in disparate ways. Bin Laden had not informed several of his own jihadist leaders about the impending attacks and so when the pendulum of catastrophe started swinging in the direction of Al-Qaeda, there was great resentment among his supporters against the group's top leaders.[82]

Two months after the attack, the host Taliban regime was decimated by the US and although Bin Laden survived the bombardment of Tora Bora, nearly 80 percent of Al-Qaeda members in Afghanistan were killed.

Abu al-Walid al-Masri, a senior leader of Al-Qaeda's inner council, later wrote that Al-Qaeda's experience in Afghanistan was "a tragic example of an Islamic movement managed in an alarmingly meaningless way." He went on, "Everyone knew that their leader was leading them to the abyss and even leading the entire country to utter destruction, but they continued to carry out his orders faithfully and with bitterness." [83]

Most of the surviving Al-Qaeda members were on the run for almost two to three years. Thus, Abu Musab Al-Suri (previously an Al-Qaeda ideologue) became criical of Bin Laden and devised his own theory of 'nizam, la tanzim' 'system, not organization,' for jihadism in order to avoid the fate of Al-Qaeda in Afghanistan.

Similarly, Abu Musab Al-Zarqawi had to abandon his activities in Herat and eventually moved to Iraq, embittered and disillusioned with the rich, Western-educated leadership of "global jihad".

Like many Salafi jihadists working with the Taliban, Al-Zarqawi had resented the practices

ISIS Ideology in Brief

ISIS's ideology originates in the branch of modern Islam (Salafism) that seeks the return of the early days of Islam (as it interprets it), rejecting later "innovations" (bida'a) in the religion which it believes corrupt its original spirit.

It condemns later Caliphates (ones that followed the rule of the first Four Pious Caliphs) and the Ottoman Empire for deviating from what it calls pure Islam and hence has been attempting to establish its own Caliphate.

Belonging to Salafi sect of Sunni Islam, this militant group of extremists believes itself to be the only correct interpreter of the Quran and considers even moderate Muslims (including Sunnis and Salafis) to be infidels. It seeks to convert all Muslims and to insure that its own bigoted and extremely violent version of Islam will dominate the world. Thus, the group is strictly against non-Muslims, Shiites and Sunni Sufis.

The ISIS believes that only a legitimate authority can undertake the leadership of jihad, and that the first priority over other areas of combat, such as fighting against non-Muslim countries, is the purification of Islamic society. For example, ISIS regards the Palestinian Sunni group Hamas as apostates (Kafir) who have no legitimate authority to lead jihad. It regards fighting Hamas as the first step toward confrontation with Israel.

of the Hanafi school of Islam followed by the local regime and did not find the Taleban regime as the ideal Islamic emirate to defend and support.[84]

Even, when he eventually founded AQI, Al-Zarqawi followed his new variant of extremism in Iraq that even Bin Laden and Al-Zawahiri found objectionable. Al-Zarqawi made Salafi-Jihadism the cornerstone of his violent ideology.

The global, pan-Islamist and anarchist approach of Al-Qaeda was replaced by a highly sectarian, 'takfeeri' (doctrine legitimizing killing of civilians on the basis of their faith) and statist approach, in which territorial control and the lust for political power became important.

Al-Zarqawi openly attacked Shiite mosques and places of worship in order to instigate sectarian wars, something even Al-Qaeda leadership found too violent and counterproductive its pan-Islamist, anti-Western campaign.

11.   The ISIS' Ideology of Caliphate, 'Takfeer' and Eschatology

However, a weakened Al-Qaeda could not afford to lose Al-Zarqawi in its hour of crisis and until his death tolerated the Iraqi brigand's recalcitrant and audacious behavior. Following his death, the AQI dismembered and lost its territories in Iraq's Sunni heartland. However, its resurgence as the ISI and ISIS in 2010, brought to the fore the same ideological dissonance with Al-Qaeda leadership, further developed and enhanced under the leadership of Abu Bakr Al-Baghadadi. These ideological divergences of the ISIS, can be categorized under the following concepts:

- *Establishment of Caliphate by Obliteration of Nation States:*

The ultimate goal of the political Islamic movement of the 20th century has been the reestablishment of the Islamic Caliphate, but not the monarchist, titular Caliphate of the Ottoman Sultan which was dismembered in 1924, but a theocratic Caliphate that is based on the Islamic rule of the Pious Caliphs during early Islamic times.

Some Islamist scholars, like Taqiuddin Nabhani, have gone to the extent of declaring that the establishment of a global, pan-Islamic Caliphate

36

"is a religious duty, "an obligation that Allah has decreed for the Muslims and commanded them to fulfill. He warned of the punishment awaiting those who neglect this duty."[85]

According to these ideologues, the concept of nation states is based on the narrow ideals of ethnic and territorial exceptionalism. The true adhesive of cohesion between all humans should be 'Tawheed' (the unity of Godhead under Islam) and Shariah (the divinely revealed Islamic law). Therefore, Islamists seek the obliteration of the "artificial borders" of nations.

However, it is the ISIS which literally stole the wind off the sails of the Islamist movement by declaring it had established the quintessential "theocratic Caliphate," and issued a map which detailed the extent of its prospective boundaries, which it said it shall conquer within a period of five years.

No previous Islamist group had ever demonstrated the brazen audacity to announce to the entire global community the establishment of the Caliphate, as that would theoretically entail the compliance of every Muslim on the globe to the Caliph and his commandments.

For a virtual unknown like Abu Bakr Al-Baghdadi, who was not even the leader of his own organization until 2010, to assume the title of the Caliph and to demand allegiance from the entire 'Ummah' (Muslim nation) was viewed as too audacious and insolent a move. As Thomas Hegghammer puts it; "For decades, restoring the caliphate has been the declared end objective of all jihadi groups, but none of them has had the audacity to declare one—until now."[86]

Therefore, the upstart Caliph and the idea of his incipient Caliphate was rejected not only by most Muslims and their governments around the world, but by almost all prominent Islamist and Jihadist organizations and their leaders, including Al-Qaeda[87].

Caliphate: A map purportedly showing the areas ISIS plans to have under its control within five years (from 2014 onwards) has been widely shared online. In addition to the Middle East, North Africa and Europe, it covers the whole of the Indian subcontinent, Central Asia and most of China, under the mythical province of Khurasan.

In fact, many strategic thinkers have wondered about the reasons behind this outrageous decision taken by the ISIS. It seems that by declaring itself a Caliphate, the ISIS proto-state has sought to capture the imagination of the newly converted Muslims around the world as well as the youth, in order to draw them into their ranks by claiming to have achieved what others could only have wished for for many years.

In fact, the ISIS taunted Al-Qaeda and the Taliban on social media of not having the courage to establish their Caliphate earlier, as they feared global Muslim backlash and rejection.

Thus, in the very first issue of its online *Dabiq* magazine it said: "If Al-Qaida and al-Taliban could not establish khilafah [caliphate] with all their power and territory for all these years, how can we expect them to suddenly unite upon haqq [truth] now? Al-Khilafah does not need them, rather, they need al-khilafah."[8]

Compared to the ISIS, Al-Qaeda never actively pursued the goal of establishing the Caliphate. Its principal stated objective has always remained to bring an end to Western occupation and military presence in

Al-Qaeda, ISIS not Islamic, but 'Khawarij'; say Islamic scholars

Tahirul Qadri Yusuf Hanson

The Islamic counter-narrative to Al-Qaeda and ISIS seems to be gathering steam. Several eminent Islamic scholars of international repute, such as Dr Tahirul Qadri, Yasir Qadhi and Yusuf Hanson, have declared jihadi organizations like Al-Qaeda and ISIS, as fulfilling the description of the infamous 'Khawarij' groups, who are prophesised in Hadeeth literature as a people that will appear in the future (on separate occasions) as outwardly religious, but will in fact be the most violent and despicable people.

According to their study, the Prophet had warned about the emergence of these "terrorist" groups and had deemed them non-Muslim and the "worst of mankind". The description in the Hadeeth describes these groups as having young and brainwashed fighters, bent on causing terror in the name of Islam.

Muslim countries and shores. The ISIS, on the other hand, has sought to upstage its parent organization by setting a loftier goal and by brazenly appointing a 'Caliph' for achieving that objective. In fact, ISIS has used the Caliphate bogey as an effective public relations gimmick to successfully grab the global spotlight and show that unlike other Islamist and jihadist movements that merely speak of establishing a Caliphate, it really means business.

• *Rise of Takfeer and Salafi-Jihadi Sectarianism in the Jihadist Narrative*

The other ideological difference between Al-Qaeda and the ISIS has been over the interpretation of the methdology of Jihadi terrorism. Whereas Al-Qaeda justified terrorism in its Jihadi warfare and regarded the death of civilians "collateral damage," ISIS makes no bones about making civilians the sole target of its attacks by openly espousing the doctrine of 'takfeer', which in its own dubious form of reasoning legitimizes the killing of a person (Muslim and non-Muslim) on account of 'apostasy'.

Thus, the targeting and killing of civilians reached a whole new level of gruesomeness under the ISIS, which even Al-Qaeda found objectionable.

According to Bernard Haykel, Professor of Near Eastern Studies and the Director of the Institute for Trans-regional Study of the Contemporary Middle East, North Africa and Central Asia at Princeton University, "For Al-Qaeda, violence is a means to an end; for ISIS, it is an end in itself"[89]

Since the time of Al-Zarqawi, Al-Qaeda and its Iraqi protege had differences over saving the 'umma' (Muslim community) from apostasy. Al-Zarqawi believed in violently purging those Muslims who do not conform to the Salafi ideals of monotheism, while Al-Zawahiri believed that it was not Muslims but the 'apostate' institutions that needed to change.[90] In fact, the unbridled excesses of Al-Zarqawi forced Al-Zawahiri and his deputy Sheikh Atiyat Allah Abdal Rahman Al-Libi[91] to write two letters in 2005 urging their Iraqi commander to bring down the violence and refrain from heavy handed enforcement of the Shariah, as it was alienating the Sunni community. "We are in a battle," Al-Zawahiri wrote, "and that more than half of this battle is taking place in the battlefield of the media."[92]

- *Apocalyptic Salafi Jihadism: Exploiting Religious 'End-Time' Narratives*

Another ideological dimension that clearly sets the ISIS apart from Al-Qaeda is its use of Islamic eschatological references (end-time prophecies) and its preponderance to find parallels in it to validate its historic role and significance to the Islamic audience. For example in July 2014, ISIS released the first two issues of *Dabiq*, a digital magazine, which is named after a Syrian town believed to be the site of a future apocalyptic battle – Islamic Armageddon (Al-Malhama Al-Kubra) - to be fought between Muslims and Romans. By projecting itself as that promised army of 'rightly guided' Muslims fighting against the West ('Romans'), as stated in Ahadeeth (sayings of the Prophet), the ISIS is cleverly using emotive propaganda to draw impressionable Muslim youth to its ranks. In fact, Abu Bakr Al-Baghdadi has repeatedly spoken of carrying out an attack on the city of Rome to initiate a war between the Christian West and Islam. The ISIS propaganda literature is replete with references to 'Ilmu Akhiru Zaman' (Islamic Knowledge of the End Times), similar to some extreme apocalyptic, mass suicide-prone Western cults of the 20th century.

According to US Gen. Martin E. Dempsey, chairman of the Joint Chiefs of Staff, the only way the ISIS seeks religious legitimacy among Muslims is by claiming to be the army which will fight the so-called Romans (i.e. the West), as mentioned in the Islamic eschatological literature. As their extremist ideology discards all classical forms of Islamic scholarship, its only legitimacy comes from its speculative claim of being the promised end-time army.

At the Aspen Institute Forum 2014, Gen. Dempsey emphasized this narrative of the ISIS, which is similar to that of several doomsday cults of the past.[93] "They actually - at least the senior leaders of ISIS - believe themselves to be the heir to the caliphate. They can only sustain that religious legitimacy if they continue to succeed. So this is not a group that can go halfway. It has to keep moving toward its ultimate end-of-days apocalyptic narrative or it will lose support because it loses religious legitimacy."

Some strategic thinkers believe that this messianic refrain of the ISIS makes it more ideologically dangerous than other jihadist and fundamentalist organizations, including Al-Qaeda. In the opening paragraph of his book *Holiest Wars,* Timothy Furnish writes: "Islamic messianic insurrections are qualitatively different from mere fundamentalist ones such as bedevil the world today, despite their surface similarities. In fact, Muslim messianic movements are to fundamentalist uprisings what nuclear weapons are to conventional ones: triggered by the same detonating agents, but far more powerful in scope and effect."[94]

According to Islamic eschatology, after lasting only a few decades in its pristine form, the true Islamic Caliphate will only be reinstated toward the end of times. Therefore, when the ISIS claims to have founded the seed-Caliphate, it is only natural for it to expand it to achieve its full geographical extent, which in theory will entail a confrontation with both the Muslim and the non-Muslim world at a global scale.

The warfare is guided by the extreme divisiveness, ruthless violence and grandiose design of establishing a global Caliphate. The difference in its ideological motivations and goals from Al-Qaeda are studied in the light of the practical strategic divergences in the warfare of Al-Qaeda and the ISIS.

Chapter Three
Organisation: Method in Madness

ISIS has many Toyota Hilux trucks that have proven more convenient than heavy tanks in the desert

12.   Forces and Weaponry

The ISIS' modus operandi is predicated on the expansion of its terrorist-cum-guerilla warfare tactics. Although its fundamental structure will always be that of a terrorist organization, US State Department Deputy Assistant Secretary for Iraq and Iran Brett McGurk has said that the ISIS is today a "full blown army".

The ISIS ranks swelled rapidly after the group's speedy territorial expansion in 2014. The total size of this terror legion has been estimated to range between the tens of thousands to over 200,000. Although in September 2004, the CIA estimated the ISIS fighters to be merely about 20,000 to 30,000 in number Russian military sources had estimated them to be in the range of 70,000, while Kurdish fighters claim their strength to be as high as 200,000.[95]

On the subject of foreign fighters, a new research by International Center for the Study of Radicalization and Political Violence (ICSR) reveals that up to 20,730 people have travelled to Syria and Iraq to fight for Sunni militant groups, mainly the ISIS/Jabhat Al Nusrah.[96] The low end of the estimate puts the figure at 16,700. It is averred that no conflict since World War II has drawn so many foreign fighters, coming from as many as 90 countries.

ISIS' FOREIGN FIGHTERS IN PROPORTION TO THEIR COUNTRY'S POPULATION

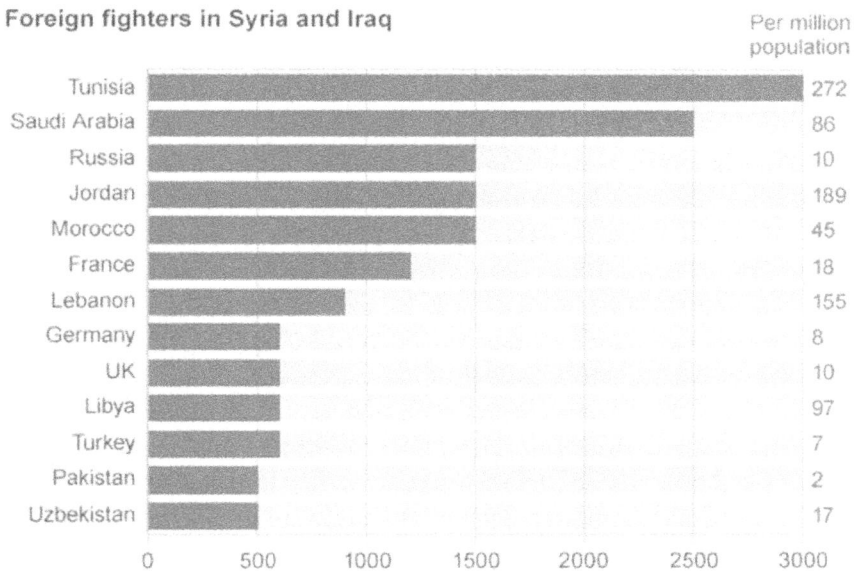

Foreign fighters in Syria and Iraq   Per million
                                                          population

Country	Per million population
Tunisia	272
Saudi Arabia	86
Russia	10
Jordan	189
Morocco	45
France	18
Lebanon	155
Germany	8
UK	10
Libya	97
Turkey	7
Pakistan	2
Uzbekistan	17

0   500   1000   1500   2000   2500   3000

Note: Upper estimates used. Countries with fewer than 500 fighters not included
Source: ICSR, CIA World Factbook

When it comes to India, officially there have been four Indian citizens (one of them dead already), who joined the ISIS in Iraq. However, according to Iraq's ambassador to India Ahmed Berwari, there may be around 20 Indians fighting for the ISIS, but their identities are not yet clear.[97] Again, it has been reported that an Indian jihadist fighting for ISIS in Iraq and Syria, who claimed to have killed at least 55 people in battle, was intercepted by Indian intelligence authorities in Turkey. During interrogation, Majeed has allegedly said he was planning to return to India as the ISIS did not pay him.[98] (c.f. Chapter Four, Section 32 titled 'The Indian Sub-Continent').

The so-called Islamic State also possesses a number of weapons systems and vehicles, including tanks and armoured fighting vehicles (BRDM2, BMP1, M111 Armoured Security Vehicle, T55, T55MV/AM/AM/AMV, MTLB, T62MK, T72/72M/A/AV/TURMS-T/M1TURMS-T, M113 APC, M1AM Abrams), field artillery, self-propelled howitzers, multiple rocket launchers (2S1Gvozdika, M18 Howitzer, BM21Grad, ZU-23-2, Type 59 Field gun), as well as an assortment of antitank guided missiles (ATGMs), anti-aircraft guns and a small number of man-portable air defense systems.

It has also been reported that the ISIS has captured and employed SA-7 and Stinger surface-to-surface missiles, M79 OSa, HJ8 and AT-4 Spigot anti-tank missiles and may have even got hands to one Scud missile of the former Ba'ath military. ISIS also captured a number of UH-60 Blackhawk helicopters and cargo planes in Mosul in June 2014.

The Syrian Observatory for Human Rights reported in October 2014 that former Iraqi pilots were training ISIS militants to fly captured Syrian jets. According to some witnesses, MiG21 and MiG-23 jets fly over al-Jarrah military airport, but the US Central Command stated that it was not aware of flights by ISIS-operated aircraft in Syria or elsewhere.[99] On 21 October 2014, the Syrian Air Force claimed that it had shot down two such aircraft over al-Jarrah air base while they were landing.[100]

According to a private weapons-tracking organization, Conflict Armament Research (CAR), ISIS forces are said to be using ammunition of United States and Chinese manufacture. These are munitions supposedly transferred by US and Chinese governments to regional actors to use against ISIS troops, which the group has captured after defeating their opponents in battle.[101]

Unlike Al-Qaeda, the ISIS strategy has been to conquer territory and continue expanding until it reaches the region dominated by Muslim countries. To this end, it has sought to control and govern territory and maintain a "cabinet of ministers," which conducts military, civil, political and financial functions.

On September 19, 2014, the British newspaper *Daily Mail* published details about the way the ISIS operates and details of its leadership hierarchy on the basis of information purportedly gathered from a USB stick found in the home of Abu Abdul Rahman Al-Bilawi, the head of ISIS' military operations in Iraq.[102]

13.   Territorial Claims: Provincial Sub-Divisions (Wilayats)

The ISIS has divided its territories in Iraq and Syria into several

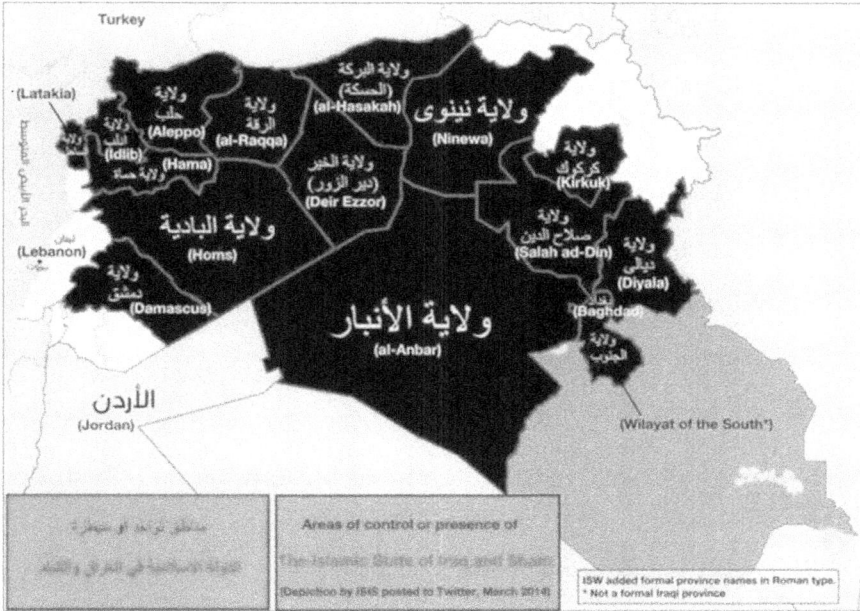

provinces, which it calls 'wilayah'. These are largely based on pre-existing provinces.[103] ISIS has also announced a new cross-border province between Iraq and Syria named Al-Furat, which spans areas of Eastern Syria and Western Anbar Province in Iraq.[104]

The group rejects the political divisions established by Western colonial powers after World War I, under the secretive Sykes-Picot Agreement.[105] Thus, the so-called Islamic State has absorbed the territories of Syria and Iraq under its control and destroyed all the signs of the borders marking the two countries. This point was made clear by Abu Bakr Al-Baghdadi, who in a message published in the magazine *Dabiq* stated: "Rush! O Muslims to your state. It is your state. Syria is not for Syrians and Iraq is not for Iraqis. The land is for the Muslims, all Muslims. This is my advice to you. If you hold to it you will conquer Rome and own the world, if Allah wills."[106]

The group's territories are currently divided into Wilayats in Iraq and Syria as follows:

Wilayahs (provinces) in Iraq (claimed but not necessarily under ISIS' control)[107]

1) Wilayat-al-Baghdad

2) Wilayat-al-Anbar

3) Wilayat-al-Diyala

4) Wilayat-al-Kirkuk

5) Wilayat-al-Salah Al-Din (and parts of Babil)

6) Wilayat-al-Fallujah (new province)

7) Wilayat-al-Dijla (new province)

8) Wilayat-al-Jazeera (new province)

Wilayahs (provinces) in Syria (claimed but not necessarily under ISIS' control):[108]

9) Wilayat-al-Barakah or Al-Hasakah

10) Wilayat-al-Khayr or Deir Ezzor

11) Wilayat-al-Raqqah

12) Wilayat-al-Badiya or Homs

13) Wilayat-al-Halab (Aleppo)

14) Wilayat-al-Idlib

15) Wilayat-al-Hama

16) Wilayat-al-Damishq (Damascus)

17) Wilayat-al-Sahel (Latakia)

18) Wilayat-al-Furat (New province straddling Iraq and Syria)

In November 2014, Abu Bakr Al-Baghdadi announced the formation of new wilayats of the ISIS, outside the Iraq and Syrian region, i.e. where the group has found new affiliates carving out spheres of influence.

Wilayats outside Syria and Iraq (claimed but not necessarily under ISIS' control) [109]

19) Wilayat-al-Barqah (in Libya)

20) Wilayat-al-Tarabalus (in Libya)

21) Wilayat-al-Fizan (in Libya)

22) Wilayat-al-Jazair (Algeria)

23) Wilayat-al-Sinai (in Egypt)

24) Wilayat-al-Sanaa (in Yemen)

25) Wilayat-al-Haramayn (Saudi Arabia)

26) Wilayat-al-Khorasan (Af-Pak region)

14. Leadership Structure

Based on intelligence-based information received over the months, international investigators have drawn a detailed picture of the ISIS' top-level leadership structure, which has over a period of time become leaner and more exclusive with Abu Bakr Al-Baghdadi at the helm. The head of the organization (which until recently was Baghdadi before his incapacitation) maintains a personal adviser or assistant (formerly Haji Bakr), and below him two immediate deputies (one for Syria and one for Iraq), an eight-member cabinet, and a military council of about 13 men.[110]

Baghdadi has tried to build his image as the Caliph on account of his apparent Ph.D. in Islamic Studies from the Islamic University of Baghdad and his background as an imam and preacher in Samarra. Though not a graduate of Al-Azhar or Dar al-Ifta' al-Masriyyah, these limited credentials places the ISIS head at a higher ecclesiastical level than even Osama bin Laden and Ayman Al-Zawahiri.[111]

Directly below the so-called Caliph/Commander of the Faithfuls (Amirul Mu'mineen) of the hierarchy come the advisory councils, such as the Sharia Council, Shura (Consultative) Council, Military (Council) and Security Council). These cover a broad range of "ministries," incorporating military, civil, political and financial duties.[112] Al-Baghdadi is also the head of the Executive Branch (Al Imara). This structure is then duplicated down the chain of command to the local level.[113] The leadership comprises of Abu Bakr Al-Baghdadi as the Caliph, his deputy Abu Suja (also known as Abdul Rahman Al Afari, who unconfirmed reports suggest died recently), Abu Muslim Al-Turkmani (also known as Fadal Ahmad Abdullah Al-Hiyali) who is charged with overseeing the Iraqi provinces, Abu Ali Al-Anbari who is Bahdadi's deputy in Syria, Abu Abdul Kadr (real name Shawkat Hazem Al Farha, general management official), and other militant leaders like the ISIS spokesman Abu Muahammad Al-Adnani, Abu Waheeb, Col. Abu Ayman Al-Iraqi, Abu Umar Al-Shisani, Mohammed Emwazi (the so-called 'Jihadi John'), among many others.

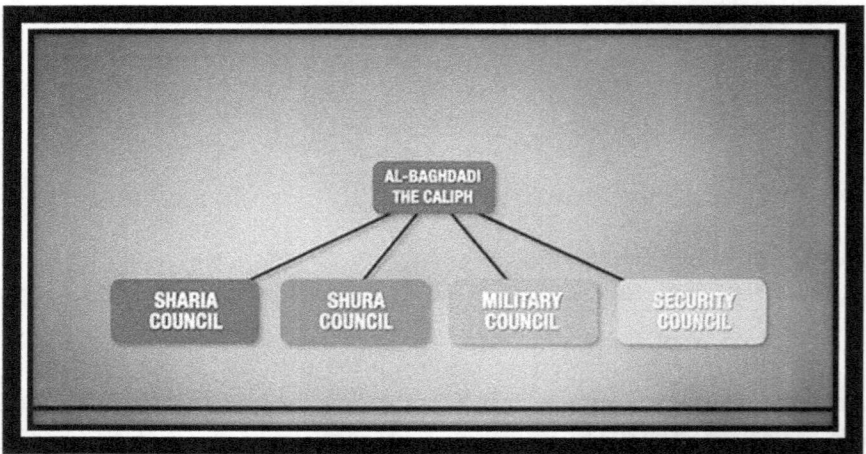

15. Bureaucracy

According to information derived from the US Department of Defense's classified Harmony Database, the ISIS' bureaucratic structure and attention to detail has allowed the group to prosper even during the toughest US counterterrorism efforts of the last decade.[114]

The ISIS today is said to be following the same **complex and detail oriented bureaucracy,** which its predecessor the ISI followed and has only become more efficient at it. Thus, when Baghdadi rose to the ISI top rung, "he had in place a sophisticated bureaucracy that was almost **obsessive about record keeping**."[115] Its 'middle-managers,' for instance, kept a detailed account of the families of the fighters to determine compensation rates upon death or capture. "They listed expenditures in neat Excel spreadsheets' that noted payments to an 'assassination platoon' and 'Al Mustafa Explosive Company'. The income from the looting of Shiite Muslim property was recorded as 'spoils'.

Reallocation and payroll costs, i.e. compensation to members and the families of deceased members were by far the largest expenses for the Islamic State, accounting for as much as 56 percent of all payouts at certain points in time, according to the documents with the US Department of Defense.

Another widely held belief that is refuted by the aforementioned financial records is that Iraqi recruits flocked to the Islamic State for higher wages and steady jobs. In fact, it turns out that the ISIS is a bad pay master. The years for which financial records are available show that the average ISIS foot soldier earns a base salary of merely $41 a month, which is much lower than the income of a brick layer who is said to make $150 a month on average.[116] According to Patrick B. Johnston of the RAND Corporation, "the salaries may have been purposely set low to ensure only committed jihadis would join the movement."[117]

16.   Funding

In spite of its affiliations with Al-Qaeda in the past, the ISIS is not entirely reliant on wealthy donors that propped up Al-Qaeda as it grew in the pre-9/11 era. Instead, the ISIS has in some ways developed a "hybrid form of funding" that is both global and local.[118]

The group has been called the richest terrorist network in history by far, making $3 million a day from oil revenues, kidnappings for ransom, sale of antiquities, human trafficking, theft and extortion. Its total worth is said to over $2 billion.[119]

According to Patrick B. Johnston from the RAND Office of External Affairs, if reports about ISIS documents seized from its senior official in Mosul are to be believed, the group's surplus runs to approximately $2 billion. Its obsession with record keeping to manage the budget may have eased as it might today be enjoying a significant surplus capital.[120]

The enormous wealth at the disposal of the ISIS has been critical behind its success in seizing territories in Syria and Iraq and in waging war on multiple fronts against various governments and several non-state armed groups. The extremist group depends on a highly complex system to control its extensive and intricate networks. In a detailed report for the magazine *Newsweek* (November issue of 2014), Janine di Giovanni, Leah McGrath Goodman, and Damien Sharkov reported that the group's currencies of choice are cash, crude oil and contraband that allow it to operate outside of legitimate banking channels.[121]

It is said to be exploiting Turkey's southern corridor, Iraq's northwestern corridor and Syria's northeastern corridor for its financing operations as they are well away from the prying eyes of international investigators. This presents a formidable challenge for the international community, which is accustomed to pursuing terrorist networks by putting pressure on established banks to expose their criminal clients. Again, the ISIS is said to have employed a large number of middlemen across the region to smuggle cash in and out of its territory. It also uses decades-old smugglers' routes (developed during the oil-for-food sanctions regime), which makes the group particularly hard to track.[122] The aforementioned *Newsweek* report states: "Highly localized and multiple revenue streams feed the terrorist organization's coffers—generating up to $6 million a day, according to Masrour Barzani, head of Kurdish Intelligence and the Kurdistan Regional Security Council." It has been reported that before ISIS captured Mosul in 2014, their total cash and assets were estimated around $875 million. After the occupation of the rich city, "with the money they robbed from banks and the value of the military supplies they looted, they could add another $1.5 billion to that (amount)."[123]

It is widely acknowledged that while some of the ISIS' funding comes from abroad, the group has largely gained virtual financial independence by taking effective control of the local economy. It is said to have taken control of resources like oil installations and refineries, in addition to food granaries in its territories in Iraq and Syria. The ISIS also makes a lot of money through criminal activities like kidnapping, extortion and taxing businesses in the region. In fact, according to Charles Lister of the Brookings Doha Center[124], the ISIS has been "almost completely self financed since at least 2005 and according to the US Department of Defense database, external funding to AQI, MSM, and ISI between 2005 and 2010 amounted to no more than five percent of its total 'income.'"

After assuming command in 2010, Baghdadi set up a financial command council and the city of Mosul gradually became the principal source of the group's income. It has been reported that by 2014, the ISIS has developed a complex extortion network that generates $12 million per month.[125]

Thus the groups main sources of revenue include:

a) Production and sale of petroleum through seized energy assets

b) Private regional and international donors

c) Extortion and taxes levies on captive population

d) Seizure of bank accounts and private assets in occupied territories

e) Ransoms from kidnappings

f) Plundering of antiquities excavated from archaeological sites

Following is the detailed study of the above mentioned sources of revenue for the ISIS:

a) Production and sale of petroleum through seized energy assets: The ISIS' oil empire stretches across an area around the size of the United Kingdom and consists of around 300 oil wells in Iraq alone, according to the latest data from the Iraq Energy Institute in Baghdad. Some of its biggest seizures include oil wells and production facilities in Hamrin (which has at least 41 oilwells, and Ajil that has 76 oilwells).

In addition, it has seized energy assets in the cities of Sfaya, Qaiyara, Najma, Jawan, Qasab, Taza and West Tikrit, according to Luay al-Khatteeb - the founder and director of the Iraq Energy Institute.[126]

FUNDING ISIS

The Islamic State of Iraq and al-Sham (ISIS) is the world's best-funded terrorist group and is richer than some small countries. How does ISIS, now controlling territory in Syria and Iraq, fill its coffers?

$ Independently Wealthy
Unlike other groups, which rely on state sponsors, major donors, or abuse of charity, ISIS is financially independent due to its successful criminal enterprise.

$ An Illegal "Inheritance"
Then known as al-Qaeda in Iraq (AQI), the group brought in some $70 million a year through criminal activities—and was so flush that central al-Qaeda asked the group for money in 2005.

$ Growing the Business
ISIS continues to engage in activities such as smuggling, extortion, and crime. Not being tied to major donors has helped the group evade counterterrorism finance measures.

$ Private Gulf Donations
Private contributions to ISIS—as well as to other groups operating in Syria, such as al-Qaeda affiliate Jabhat al-Nusra—are a concern for U.S. policy makers. Wealthy citizens and others in the Persian Gulf countries have fun ne led hundreds of millions into the conflict.

$ U.S. Response
Washington can tighten counter-terrorism financing cooperation with Saudi Arabia and other Gulf states, but significantly undermining ISIS's financial base would now require rolling back its access to local Syrian and Iraqi income sources.

ENTERPRISING CRIMINALS
» Extortion
ISIS levies around $8 million per month in "taxes" on local businesses
» Kidnapping
» Robberies
The seizure of Mosul's central bank netted tens of millions of dollars
» Counterfeiting
» Smuggling
Oil, weapons, and antiquities
» Racketeering

Sources
• Declaring an Islamic State, Running a Criminal Enterprise
• Qatar and ISIS Funding: The U.S. Approach
• Saudi Funding of ISIS
• The Terrorist Funding Disconnect with Qatar and Kuwait

ALL IN THE NEIGHBORHOOD: GULF FUNDING

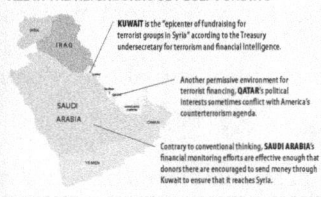

KUWAIT is the "epicenter of fundraising for terrorist groups in Syria" according to the Treasury undersecretary for terrorism and financial intelligence.

Another permissive environment for terrorist financing, QATAR's political interests sometimes conflict with America's counterterrorism agenda.

Contrary to conventional thinking, SAUDI ARABIA's financial monitoring efforts are effective enough that donors there are encouraged to send money through Kuwait to ensure that it reaches Syria.

Source: The Washington Institute for Near East Policy

At its peak over the summer of 2014, ISIS operated around 350 oilwells in Iraq, says Al-Khatteeb. However, in the battles with the Kurdish peshmerga forces and coming under fire from U.S.-led airstrikes which began in August 8, it has at least lost around 45 of these oilfields and facilities—including in Ain Zala and Butma—and it has torched a few of the oilwells as it pulled out. In both locations, the Peshmerga recaptured the oilwells with a total output of around 15,000 barrels a day.[127]

The remaining wells in Iraq under ISIS control have a combined production capacity of 80,000 barrels a day—a fraction of Iraq's total production of around 3 million barrels a day. By contrast, ISIS possesses about 60 percent of Syria's total production capacity, which, before the civil war kicked into high gear, produced around 385,000 barrels a day, according to the Iraq Energy Institute. ISIS does not appear to have access to working oil pipelines, and it lacks the expertise to maintain its oilfields for any length of time. In Syria, oilfields under its control are more mature, requiring greater extraction skills, compared with the higher-yielding fields in Iraq.

According to a report in *Wall Street Journal,* by late August 2014, the ISIS was selling as much as 70,000 barrels of oil daily from Syria and Iraq (at $26-$35 per barrel of heavy oil and $60 per barrel of light crude) to internal black market customers and external buyers in Iraq, Lebanon, Turkey and Kurdistan.[128] These calculations add up to a daily income of around $1-3 million, which over 12 months amounts to $365 million-$1.1 billion.[129]

However, analysts like Charles Lister opine that since the targeting of oil facilities in Syria since late-September 2014, the oil revenues would have dropped considerably. In any case, ISIS is still able to produce only around a fifth of its oilfields' total capacity in Iraq and Syria because of technical issues. Therefore the group is probably being helped by its oil-rich neighbors, Al-Khatteeb alleges. The US Department of the Treasury's Undersecretary for Terrorism and Financial Intelligence David Cohen also holds a similar view and has stated that despite their hostility to ISIS, the Kurds in Iraq, Turkey and Syria have all done deals with the group, often through middlemen.

b) Private regional and international donors

The extensive research conducted by the *Newsweek* magazine mentioned above concluded with some bold pronouncements about the continued role of donors particularly in the Gulf countries of Saudi, Arabia, Kuwait and Qatar in swelling the coffers of the ISIS. The report states that "grossing as much as $40 million or more over the past two years, ISIS has accepted funding from government or private sources in the oil-rich nations of Saudi Arabia, Qatar and Kuwait—and a large network of private donors, including Persian Gulf royalty, businessmen and wealthy families."[130]

Until recently, all three countries openly donated hefty sums to rebel groups fighting Bashar Assad's Syrian regime, with ISIS being among them. Only after much persuasion by former Secretary of State Hillary Clinton and the international community did Saudi Arabia pass legislation in 2013 which criminalized financial support of terrorist organizations such as Al-Qaeda, Jabhat Al-Nusrah and ISIS.

According to the investigators, some of the donations were "routinely laundered" through unregistered charities in the form of 'humanitarian aid,' with terrorists coordinating geographical drop-off points using social media websites through cell phone applications like What'sApp and Kik. The US Treasury Department alleges that the Al-Ajmi family of Sunni clerics in Kuwait lie at the center of Islamist fund-raising efforts for extremists. It particularly suspects Sheikh Shafi Al-Ajmi, for channelling funds to ISIS militants.[131]

"Through fund raising appeals on social media and the use of financial networks, Shafi al-Ajmi, Hajjaj al-'Ajmi, and al-'Anizi have been funding the terrorists fighting in Syria and Iraq," David Cohen has reportedly stated.[132]

The name of other suspects in this regard are Nazim Al-Misbah, Ajeel Al-Nashmi, Nabil Al-Awadi, Nayef Al-Ajmi and Mohammed Al-Ajmi.[133]

The report also accuses the supposed 'ring-leaders' of the 'humanitarian' and other fund-raising movements to include Qatar-based Tariq bin Al-Tahar Al-Harzi (who allegedly raised $2 million from Qatari funders that went "straight" to the ISIS) and another Qatari citizen Salim Hasan Khalifa Rashid al-Kuwari for securing "hundreds of thousands of dollars" for ISIS, as well as acting as the financier for the terror group's Iraqi affiliates. The US Treasury Department also calls Professor al-Nuaymi "a Qatar-based terrorist financier and facilitator who has provided money and material support and conveyed communications to al-Qa'ida and its affiliates in Syria, Iraq, Somalia and Yemen for more than a decade. He was considered among the most prominent Qatar-based supporters of Iraqi Sunni extremists."[134]

ജോൽ

It is believed that almost 6 million euros were paid for the release of three Spanish aid workers held captive by the ISIS, followed by a reported $18 million for four French journalists, and substantial payments for an Italian aid worker, and a Danish photojournalist, who was released after the family apparently raised the money for the ransom

ജോൽ

According to Masrour Barzani, head of Kurdish Intelligence and the Kurdistan Regional Security Council, ISIS is currently receiving enough steady supplies of funds to sustain itself for the foreseeable future, as "many people who believe in these extremist ideologies believe it is their duty to donate."[135]

c) Extortion and taxes levied on captive population

Extortion has long been one of the ISIS' most lucrative revenue sources. Until early 2009, for example, ISI documents reveal that in Mosul it was making roughly the same share of revenue from extortion as from oil.[136] Even in areas not under its full control, ISIS is said to maintain extortion networks and protection rackets. The ISIS fighters are known to have imposed shadow taxation in areas under their control and since the proclamation of the caliphate an official taxation system has been reportedly introduced. According to Charles Lister, "The organized taxation system targets trucks transporting food and electronics from Syria and Jordan via Iraq's Al-Waleed and Al-Tanif crossings."

As of September 2014, rates were placed at $300 per truck of foodstuffs and $400 per load of electronic goods, with an occasional $800 flat rate for trucks in general."[137] This collection of taxes is done remarkably professionally. According to Mitchell Prothero: "Not only does the ISIS offer protection from bandits, but its tax collectors also provide traders with paperwork that shows they've paid IS taxes as well as counterfeit government tax receipts that truckers can show Iraqi Army checkpoints, which allow them to pass without further payments."[138] The ISIS has imposed the jizya (tax on non-Muslims) ranging from $250 to "large sums". The group threatens to kill Christians or seize their property if they fail to pay the fee.[139]

d) Seizure of bank accounts and private assets in occupied territories

When the ISIS captured the city of Mosul in the summer of 2014, it not only seized a huge amount of abandoned military hardware, but also raided the city's central bank and took off with about $425 million. However, the news was later claimed to be false with Borzou Daragahi of the *Financial Times* reporting that the story was unconfirmed and highly unlikely, according to the CEO of Iraq's United Bank for Investment, Alaa Karam Allah. "Nobody until now has confirmed that story," Atheel al-Nujaifi, governor of Nineveh province which includes Mosul, told the *Financial Times*.[140] The group is also infamous for seizing the properties of members of the Shiite, Christian and even Yazidi and Turkmen communities as well as the assets of opposing Sunni groups.

e)   Ransoms from kidnappings

The group is also known for its efficient kidnap-for-ransom operations. While hostage taking has proven to be a useful business through the public execution of American and British nationals, the kidnappings are also done for securing ransoms for other captives. According to Simon Critchley, the first major catch of Western hostages for the ISIS was when the group gathered together 23 of them from 12 countries, the majority of them Europeans during the initial period of civil war in Syria.

Later, they grabbed 46 Turks and three Iraqis during the fall of Mosul in June 2014. These were held in captivity under the Children's Hospital in Aleppo and subsequently transferred to Raqqa in eastern Syria, the present capital of the ISIS. Although the two US and three British hostages – James Foley, Steven Sotloff, David Haines and Alan Henning, Peter Kassig – were horrifically beheaded between August and November last year and a Russian captive (Sergey Gorbunov) shot dead earlier, the several continental Europeans returned home safely because their governments negotiated their release.

Critchley adds: "Details are murky, but it would appear that, from among the twenty-three, almost 6 million euros was paid for the release of three Spanish aid workers, followed by a reported $18 million for four French journalists, and substantial payments for an Italian aid worker, and a Danish photojournalist, who was released after the family apparently raised the money for the ransom. (It should also be noted that, according to press reports, the forty-six Turkish hostages and the three Iraqis may have been released in a prison swap for 180 Islamic militants—including two British jihadists, Shabazz Suleman and Hisham Folkard, being held by Turkish authorities. President Erdogan of Turkey denied that any ransom had been paid, but was rather cagey about the details of the negotiations.)"[141]

The US and British governments have adhered to a two-fold strategy when dealing with ISIS ransom demands: a media blackout and an firm refusal to pay, other countries have not always been so strict.

Although French and Spanish authorities deny paying ransom money to free their citizens, several independent investigators assert both countries paid considerable amount to free their countrymen (with France said to have paid $14 million ransom for the release of four journalists).

56

Thus, ransoms from kidnappings reportedly make up about 20 percent of ISIS's revenue, says Sajad Jiyad of the London based think tank London-based think tank Integrity.

The US Treasury estimates ISIS has received $20 million in ransoms until late 2014. "If a ransom is paid, the person is freed—if not, he or she is killed. Sometimes ISIS forces allow victims to telephone their families to report that they are being tortured, in the hope of raising a large ransom to secure their freedom."[142]

One needs also add here the number of kidnappings of women who were then forced into marriage or sold for sex is around 4,000 Yazidi women and girls—not including children—and "more than that from the Shia-Turkoman minorities."[143] India managed to successfully free 46 Indian nurses from ISIS captivity in July last year, the fate of 39 Indian workers under ISIS custody is still unclear.

f) Plundering of antiquities excavated from archaeological sites

Another major economic resource for the ISIS is the growing loot and sale of Iraqi and Syrian antiquities as the countries have a rich history of civilization. In fact, looting (often with bulldozers) is now the ISIS' second-largest source of finance after oil, Western intelligence officials say.[144] It is estimated that ISIL raises US$200 million a year from cultural looting.[145]

The war has destroyed ancient cities such as Nimrud, Homs and Aleppo. Perhaps the greatest loss has been the destruction of the ancient cities of Nimrud and Hatra.[146] On March 6, 2015, Reuters reported that IS "fighters have looted and bulldozed the ancient Assyrian city of Nimrud in their latest assault on some of the world's greatest archaeological and cultural treasures".[147]

Nimrud, about 20 miles (30 km) south of Mosul, was built around 1250 BC. Four centuries later it became capital of the neo-Assyrian empire - at the time the most powerful state on Earth, extending to modern-day Egypt, Turkey and Iran.

Meanwhile, residents near the archeological city of Hatra in northern Iraq have told Iraqi officials that ISIS militants had brought bulldozers to the site after two large explosions went off one morning in early March, 2015. Kurdish official Saeed Mamuzini also claimed witnesses saw the militants "carrying away artifacts from Hatra," just two days before they destroyed the city.[148]

Thus, Roman, Greek, Babylonian and Assyrian sites are devastated by fighting and looting, and five of the six UNESCO World Heritage sites in Syria have been seriously damaged.[149] Statues, artworks, shrines, manuscripts, ancient figurines, seals and coins are fuelling a multi-million dollar trade in precious relics that are making way to collectors in Gulf countries as well as through Turkey into Europe.

British MP Robert Jenrick has raised concerns over reports about ISIS demanding a 20 per cent cut on all sales of antiquities stolen by private individuals. In this respect, social activists and politicians in the US and Britain are calling for a UN Security Council resolution that opposes the trade in stolen antiquities, and the Hague Convention protecting cultural properties during war. [150] In an extreme display of Wahabi puritanism, the ISIS destroyed the tomb and shrine of Prophet Yunus (Jonah in Christianity) in July 2014,, the 13th century mosque of Imam Yahya Abu Al-Qassimin, the 14th century shrine of Prophet Jerjis (St. George to Christians) and attempted the destruction of the Hadba minaret at the 12th century Great Mosque of Al-Nuri.

In late May 2015, ISIS entered the ancient Syrian city of Palmyra and it is feared that it would rampage its artifacts and make billions by selling them in the black market. However, ISIS has said it will not destroy or bulldoze the ancient monuments of Palmyra, but will destroy the statues because of religious reasons.[151]

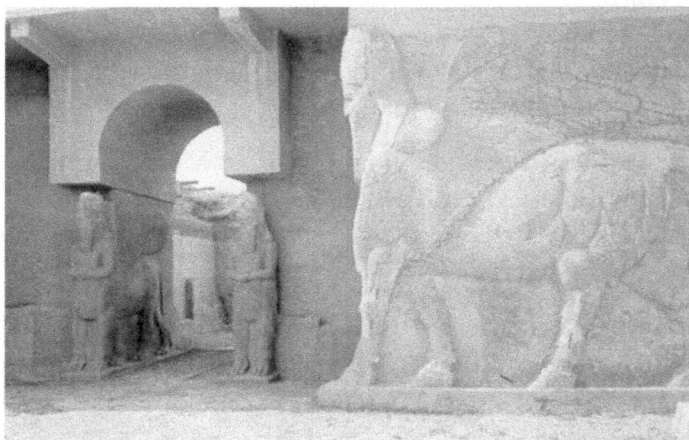

One of the gateways into the ancient city of Nimrud now destroyed by ISIS

In January 2015, an ISIS religious leader Naji Abdullah from Mosul, gave an interview to the Al-Araby Al-Jadeed outlet and claimed that the group had an annual budget of $2 billion for 2015 and an estimated surplus of $250 million surplus.[152] He claimed that the ISIS is using this surplus to develop and expand its so-called 'Caliphate' in Iraq and Syria. Another religious figure in Mosul, Sheikh Abu Saad Al-Ansari, had earlier claimed that the budget would help alleviate poverty, treat the disabled and the families of the ISIS fighters.

Along with the budget, the group is also said to have opened its own bank, called the 'Islamic Bank', where customers can not only receive loans but also deposit their money.

Earlier in November, ISIS reportedly announced plans to mint its own currency in pure gold, silver and copper material. The statement issued by the 'Dar Al-Mal' (something like a finance ministry) stated that the currency will include seven coins: two gold, three silver and two copper.[153] The name of the gold currency will be called 'dinar', the silver 'dirham' and the copper 'falasa'.

عملات دولة الخلافة الإسلامية

The ISIS' new currencies as released by Diwan al-Mal ((an equivalent of a present-day ministry of finance) Falasa (copper) Dirham (Silver) Dinar (Gold)

17.   Administration and Governance

With its proclamations of becoming the model Islamic state and then the much vaunted Caliphate, the ISIS has raised idealized expectations of governance for its supporters in the Middle East. Therefore, it has placed upon itself the "fundamental dilemma" that most jihadis face: "They cannot attain their goal if they don't govern, yet the record shows them repeatedly failing at governance efforts."[154]

However, thus far the ISIS has been able to sustain satisfactory levels of governance, with local citizens living under its rule describing its administration as "fast and efficient" with "everything coordinated (and all) parts of the administration are linked, (they share information and in general seem good at working together)."[155]

Available evidence shows that the ISIS has managed to administer with some level of competence rural and urban areas under its control. "Through the integration of military and political campaigns, particularly in the provincial capital of Raqqa, ISIS has built a holistic system of governance that includes religious, educational, judicial, security, humanitarian, and infrastructure projects, among others."[156]

The city of Raqqa is the central city or headquarters in the ISIS' territorial network, some observers even call it the capital of the so-called Islamic State. The city offers "the most developed example" of the ISIS' administration and its vision of the Caliphate. Other cities like Mosul, Al Bab and Manjib in the province of Aleppo also provide us with a detailed picture of the group's administrative methods.

The ISIS has two facets to its governance: administrative and service-oriented. In the administrative sphere, the organization's offices manage religious enforcement, courts and punishment, educational programs (which are mainly religious in orientation) and public relations.

In the initial stages, while in the process of establishing full control of a newly seized territory, the ISIS first establishes outreach centers and rudimentary court systems, mainly because they are less resource intensive and less controversial among the population. Having consolidated militarily, the ISIS then puts in place religious police, harsh punishments, and its own version of education. These types of programs entail dedicated personnel, greater resource investments and support from large sections of the population.[157]

The seizure of Mosul provides a good example of this incremental approach toward administrative consolidation. A day after the capture of the city on June 9-10, 2014, the ISIS released its 'wathiqat al-madina' (charter of the city) on June 12, which in 16 points outlined the new law of the land.[158] Initially, the ISIS displayed bold shows of military power to enforce a perception of authority and sought to encourage mass surrender of armed men in "repentance offices" set up by the ISIS.

Central to the group's governance is the implementation of a strict form of Shariah. "This includes the imposition of hudud (fixed Islamic punishments for serious crimes); enforcing attendance of the five daily prayers; banning drugs, alcohol and tobacco; controlling personal appearance, including clothing; forbidding gambling and gender mixing; and ordering the destruction of religious shrines, among other rules."[159]

The ISIS has also imposed the 'dhimmi' (protection) pact on non-Muslims in its cities, so long as they regularly pay jizya (poll tax) and other regulations such as not building additional places of worship for their community, removal of all visible signs of their faith, not carrying weapons, and not selling or consuming pork or liquor.[160] In fact, the ISIS issued an ultimatum to northern Iraq's dwindling Christian population to either convert to Islam, pay a religious levy or face death within 48 hours, according to a statement distributed in Mosul in July last year. The statement said: "We offer them (Iraqi Christians) three choices: Islam; the dhimma contract - involving payment of jizya; if they refuse this they will have nothing but the sword."[161] Thereafter, the insurgents painted the properties of Christians and Shia members of the Shabak and Turkmani communities with the Arabic letters 'noon' (indicating nasrani sect of Christians) and 'ra' (rafida term denoted for the Shiite) respectively.[162] It is reported that following such harassment, the vast majority of Christians and Shiite in the city fled within a week. The treatment of the ISIS of the Yazidi community, a so-called non-monotheistic faith, has been even more "uncompromising". In October 2014, the ISIS labeled Yazidis as Satanists, thereby making members of the community legitimate for enslavement and allowed their women to be made concubines of their fighters.[163] The ISIS also has police forces (both male and female) that are formed and deployed to patrol the streets and enforce traditional civil and sharia laws. It is reported that as many as 60 British women have joined an all-female

Sharia police unit of the ISIS, known as Al-Khansa Brigade in Raqqa, to help expose among other things male activists who attempt to disguise themselves in women's clothing to avoid detention.[164]

The ISIS reportedly spends a lot of resources on social services, like managing humanitarian aid, bakeries, and running infrastructure such as electricity, gas and water lines. ISIS also tries to manage large industrial facilities, such as dams and thermal power plants. It frequently subsidizes the price of staple products, particularly bread and has been known to put a cap on rent prices.[165]

In addition, civilian bus services are run generally for free, postal services are established, free vaccination and healthcare are offered, soup kitchens are established for the poor, loans are provided for construction projects, Islam-oriented schools are opened for boys and girls, and Raqqa even has a consumer protection office that closes shops for selling poor quality products.[166] It is this stick-and-carrot approach that has largely kept the public tacitly content with the ISIS rule and when combined with the group's vast financial resources has allowed it to develop a form of governance.

Chapter FOUR
Warfare: Terror for Territory

ISIS engages in one of the most brutal forms of warfare known in recent history

18. ISIS' Strategic Divergence with Al-Qaeda

As noted above, relations between Bin Laden and Al-Zarqawi, followed by those of Al-Zawahiri and Al-Baghdadi had always remained tense until the two sides severed links in 2014.

Although differences in personality and power struggle had a large part to play in the disaffiliation of the ISIS with Al-Qaeda, there are also major ideological and strategic issues that led to the parting of ways.

While Al-Qaeda positioned itself as the overarching, global jihadist movement that supported various Sunni insurgencies around the world, its legitimacy and competence of leading the global jihadist movement was put to question by many of its affiliates, fighting almost independently on their several, disparate fronts.

The AQI and the ISIS, under the dynamic leaderships of Al-Zarqawi and Al-Baghdadi respectively, developed a highly potent and dangerous force, which even Al-Qaeda central found difficult to manage and control. Over time, the ISIS ideology became more indiscriminately violent, parochial, sectarian and millenarian. Finally it sought to upstage the utopian dream of every jihadist organization since mid-20th century, by declaring the establishment of the Caliphate in direct opposition to the modern global political system.

a) *Non-Territorial, Anarchist Al-Qaeda Versus Statist, Expansionist ISIS:*

Perhaps the biggest difference in the strategic approach and outlook toward the realization of a violent Islamist overthrow of the current geopolitical order in the Middle East region and then the world between Al-Qaeda and the ISIS is that whereas Al-Qaeda has devised the strategy of waging a diffuse, asymmetric, world-wide campaign of terror to destabilize the Western powers and their so-called 'collusive regimes' in the Muslim world to the point of their eventual exhaustion and collapse, the ISIS has opted to first gain power and control

Al-Qaeda versus ISIS: Strategic Divergences

- Difference over on-field (ISIS) vs behind-the-scenes leadership (Al-Qaeda)

- Al-Qaeda is sophisticated terrorist organization, ISIS 4GW military force

- Non-territorial, anarchist warfare of Al-Qaeda versus statist expansionism of ISIS' Caliphate

- Mainly anti-West campaign of Al-Qaeda versus the apocalyptic agenda of Baghdadi's Brigades

- Al-Qaeda Seeks Overthrow of Regimes, ISIS aims to purge communities

- Territory-based ISIS gives precedence to the immediate and 'Near Enemy' (Shiite Iraq and Alawiite Assad regime), as opposed to Al-Qaeda's 'Far Enemies' (US, EU and Israel) over a territory (in their case Iraq and Syria that have an eschatological significance), with the intent of then expanding it to ultimately cover the entire Muslim world and thereby fulfill the legitimacy of its claim to Caliphate.

b) *Spat Over On-Field Versus Remote Leadership*

There are also differences over the styles of leadership between the ISIS and Al-Qaeda, which can be traced back to some of the ideological differences between Bin Laden and Al-Zarqawi during their association in Afghanistan in the late 1990s. In fact, both organizations come from different backgrounds and outlooks. The two merely formed a marriage of convenience in 2004, but strains in the relationship existed since mid-1990s.

At that time, Al-Zarqawi operated in Herat, "on the other side of Afghanistan"[167] and had "a largely distinct, if occasionally overlapping, agenda"[168] with al-Qaeda. Even at that time, Al-Zarqawi wanted to run his own training camp in Herat with his personal followers who had just been released in a Jordanian prison amnesty earlier in the year. However, Al-Zarqawi found it difficult to set up his camp, and it was on the intervention of the Al-Qaeda militant Saif el-Adel that Al-Zarqawi was given a small amount of seed money by Osama bin Laden, which helped him set up his base.[169] In fact, Bin Laden wanted to co-opt Al-Zarqawi by requesting a 'baya' (religious oath of allegiance), but this overture was repeatedly rebuffed by Al-Zarqawi.

Whereas Bin Laden and his followers came from at least the upper middle class and had studied at the university level, Al-Zarqawi and his band of ex-convicts came from poor, less educated backgrounds. In addition, Al-Zarqawi's criminal past and his views on 'takfeer' caused a major friction and suspicion between the two sides.

However, the biggest point of contention between the two leaderships arose over the precedence of the behind-the-scenes management of Bin Laden and Al-Zawahiri over Zarqawi's 'on-the-battlefront' brand of leadership.[170]

Al-Zarqawi argued that the upper echelons of the Al-Qaeda were too far away from the real battle fronts to properly lead the so-called jihadi battles and that leaders fighting on the battleground, like himself, should have greater freedom to carry out their campaigns. Al-Qaeda leadership, however, found this line of thinking as dangerous and unacceptable and even Al-Zarqawi's own ideological mentor, Sheikh Abu Muhammad Al-Maqdisi, severed relations with his protégé on this matter.

c) *State Caliphate of ISIS versus Pan-Jihadism of Al-Qaeda*

One of the most important ways in which ISIS differs from Al-Qaeda is that it does not want to operate as a shadowy jihadist network, but wants to rule over the territory it occupies as the Caliphate of the Muslim world.

Its audacity to ask Muslims of the world to regard a hitherto unknown militant — the ISIS leader Abu Bakr Al-Baghdadi — as the Caliph of the Islamic world, has been vilified and condemned by Muslims around the world and even by leaders of several jihadist outfits and Al-Qaeda.

For its part, in the very first edition of its online magazine *Dabiq*, ISIS implicitly criticized Al-Qaeda among other jihadist groups of continuing with their individual campaigns, even when the Khilafah (i.e. the so-called ISIS' Caliphate) has been established.

"Sadly, they (ISIS fighters) are now opposed by the present leadership of famous jihad groups who have become frozen in the phase of nikayah attacks (initial disruptive campaigns), almost considering the attainment of power to be taboo or destructive. And rather than entrusting the affairs of the Ummah to the pious mujahidin (ISIS fighters), the present heads of these groups insist upon leaving the matter out for grabs so that any munafiq (hypocrite) can stretch out his arm and reach for the leadership of the Ummah (the Pan-Islamic Nation) only to destroy it."[171]

Unlike, the Al-Qaeda that works in the shadows and provides funding, military training and strategic support to various terrorist organizations in the Middle East and around the world, the ISIS rules independently over a territory encompassing millions of people. It has outwitted every jihadist organization's dream of establishing an Islamic Khilafah by declaring the area under its control the center of the Islamic world and now it wants to expand its territory (based in Iraq and Syria) to all the regions inhabited by Muslims. Thus, ISIS has tied its legitimacy to territory, whereas Al-Qaeda continues to be a largely ideological and spectral menace, aiding and abetting terror around the world.

By controlling and governing a large expanse of territory, the ISIS has evolved from a terror outfit into a proto-state with security and administrative responsibilities and the onus of putting its version of Sharia rule into practice. By calling itself the Caliphate, it has raised the stakes for itself. To gain legitimacy in the eyes of Muslims around the world, it has to keep expanding and at the same time provide an ideal administration and security to people within its territory to establish its claim of being a legitimate Caliphate.

d) *Priority of 'Near Enemy' Over 'Far Enemy' for ISIS*

As the ISIS is bound to a territory, it is natural that its enemies in the immediate vicinity gain precedence over what it perceives as the distant foes, viz. Israel and the West, who are regarded as Islam's arch enemy by almost all Muslim fundamentalist organizations in the world. Thus, ISIS regards the Shiite-dominated regimes of Damascus and Baghdad as the vilest and most pernicious of its enemies, which also conforms with its takfeeri ideology (which regards hypocritical Muslims as a greater enemy than non-Muslims).

Whereas Al-Qaeda's intent is to keep attacking the Far Enemy the United States and its allies and then to exhaust their armies by engaging them in asymmetric warfare, ISIS wants to violently purge Muslim state and non-state actors that do not follow its version of quintessential Islam before launching jihad on non-Muslim adversaries.[172]

Thus, ISIS regards the Palestinian Sunni group Hamas as an apostate group, which has misled the Muslim world by claiming to lead jihad. It considers fighting and eliminating Hamas as the first step toward confrontation with Israel.[173]

e) *Al-Qaeda Targets Regimes, ISIS Attacks Communities*

It might be difficult to comprehend but Al-Qaeda leaders have often complained about the savagery and violence perpetrated by the ISIS forces in Iraq and Syria, particularly its brutality toward Sunnis themselves. One can trace back this frustration to 2005, when Al-Zawahiri and Sheikh Atiyat

Allah Abd al-Rahman al-Libi, a senior al-Qaeda ideologue and operations leader (who was killed in a drone attack in 2011), issued stern warnings to Al-Zarqawi in two separate letters to tone down the violence and the "over-the-top enforcement of sharia,"[174] which they argued was alienating Sunnis and hurting the long-term goals of the global jihadist project. In fact, Al-Zawahiri urged Al-Zarqawi to remember "that we are in a battle, and that more than half of this battle is taking place in the battlefield of the media."[175]

Again, whereas ISIS believes that the only way to save the 'umma' (global Muslim community) from its present ills is to purge it from the influence of 'apostate' beliefs and sects, Al-Qaeda finds the problem instead in 'apostate' institutions and not sects that need to be changed.[176] This has amounted to "a more strategic versus doctrinaire outlook, as well as differing attitudes toward the role of institution building and governance."[177]

In fact, Al-Qaeda's concerns over the pursuance of takfeeri ideology even against the Sunni community by the ISIS and the Tehrik-i-Taliban Pakistan have been confirmed in the letters seized in Abbotabad, following the US special forces raid against Bin Laden. Again, in September 2013, Al-Zawahiri released a pamphlet titled "General Guidelines for the Work of a Jihadi," which codifies the rules of violence and engagement for an Al-Qaeda fighter, in an attempt to control the worsening jihadist violence, particularly against the Sunni community.[178] In the recent fighting between ISIS and Jabhat Al-Nasrah (Al-Qaeda's affiliate in Syria), prominent jihadist ideologues Abu Qatada Al-Filistini, Iyad Qunaybi, Hani Al-Sibai and more importantly Abu Muhammad Al-Maqdisi (the former mentor of Al-Zarqawi) have condemned ISIS' violence and disavowed it.

Al-Maqdisi has also rejected ISIS' classification of Shiites as nonbelievers, and in an interview to Al-Jazeera[179] said that he did not consider ordinary Shiites as non-Muslims, and therefore it was "forbidden to equate the ordinary Shiite with the American in warfare." Even Bin Laden's attitude toward the Shiite and Iran (the country ruled by Shiite Islamic clerics) was more nuanced. He favored tactical cooperation with the Shiites and his son Saad bin Laden reportedly lived in Iran for several years under very light house arrest.[180] On the other hand, the ISIS considers the

Shiite sect as their principal enemy, against whom they are fighting both in Iraq and Syria. It can be argued that the Shiite have emerged as the biggest foe of the ISIS, partly because of its Iraq-centric military operations, as opposed to Al-Qaeda's globalist jihadist ideology.

Thus, Al-Qaeda generally targets state institutions and power centers of a regime. The ISIS, however, has a medieval axe to grind against people belonging to various religions and sects and does not mind targeting such populations per se. For instance, it does not mind blowing up Sunni Kurdish population in Kobane, or Sunni villages that lie on its way to attacking the Shiite dominated town of Samarra. Therefore, it has no qualms about ethnically cleansing Yazidis and Christians, even as the Al-Qaeda affiliated Jabhat Al-Nusrah has reportedly exercised relative restraint in this regard.

f) *Fundamentalist Al-Qaeda Versus Apocalyptic ISIS Ideology*

To the ISIS, Iraq is central to its global jihadist aspirations. It follows Al-Zarqawi's thinking of waging and winning a jihad in Iraq as central because "if jihad fails in Iraq, the [Muslim] nation will never rise again."[181]

Around this premise, ISIS has developed an apocalyptic myth of the end-of-days jihad to be waged against the so-called 'Romans' in certain Hadith literature around the town of *Dabiq* in Syria. Thus, ISIS wants to lure the West to Syria to wage that battle and consecrate itself as the righteous Islamist force. Al-Qaeda has not till date made any such eschatological claims to its jihad and has a global jihadist ideology, which is not particularly linked to a particular area, based on its importance in eschatological literature. Thus, the US occupation of Iraq and Syria, theatres of future wars in Islamic apocalyptic literature, has added to the mythical lore and appeal of the ISIS, even as Al-Qaeda has refrained from aligning itself to any eschatological claims till date. To Al-Qaeda the defeat of Western powers and the removal of so-called corrupt regimes seems more important than the imagined glory of a prospective Islamic Caliphate.

'Architect of Global Jihad'

Abu Musab Al-Suri

Born as Mustafa Setmariam Nasar in Aleppo (Syria) c. 1958, Al-Suri is currently incarcerated in a Syrian prison. He is regarded as "the most articulate exponent of modern jihad and its most sophisticated strategies".

Al-Suri was once a close Bin Laden aide, but eventually advocated "leaderless jihad" in his online book 'Call to Global Islamic Resistance'. It's a treatise on 'lone wolf' operations and eschatological propaganda that the ISIS has apparently learnt a lot from. In 1987, Al-Suri fell in love with and married Spanish lady, Elena Moreno.

19. Formative Influences on ISIS' Warfare of Dissident Al-Qaeda Strategists

Much of the ISIS literature pertaining to its strategy and warfare borrows heavily from Al-Qaeda ideologues,[182] many of whom disapproved of the leadership policies of Osama bin Laden and Ayman Al-Zawahiri, following the US war in Afghanistan after the 9/11 attacks. Prominent among these jihadists and ideologues are Abu Musab Al-Suri, Abu Muhammad Al-Maqdisi and Abu Musab Al-Zarqawi.[183]

This internal dissension and criticism within Al-Qaeda arose after overwhelming US response to September 11 attacks in which the Taliban regime (which had given sanctuary to Al-Qaeda fighters) was routed and US airstrikes heavily pounded Al-Qaeda fighters in Tora Bora. Although Bin Laden and some members of the top leadership escaped the attacks about 80 percent of Al-Qaeda is said to have been decimated. In addition, Al-Qaeda's terrorist strikes were condemned around the world, including Muslim countries which criticized the September 11 strikes as being contrary to Islam.[184]

A senior leader of Al-Qaeda's inner council, Abu Al-Walid Al-Masri later observed that the most serious issue for Al-Qaeda's experience in Afghanistan was "the extreme weakness of Bin Laden's political and military capabilities." He added: "This was no longer a secret as Bin Laden revealed this himself in his own statements, which he released after leaving Afghanistan, most notably in his first statement after the Tora Bora battle, which revealed his gross ignorance of the fundamental principles of military action."[185]

a) *Abu Musab Al-Suri's Book 'Call to Global Islamic Resistance'*

Another dissenting voice within Al-Qaeda is that of Abu Musab Al-Suri, a Syrian ideologue who was part of Al-Qaeda's inner council.

It was Al-Suri who introduced CNN's reporter Nicholas Bergen to Bin Laden for the now-famous first interview of the Al-Qaeda leader back in 1997. At that time, Bergen described Suri as an impressive person.

"He was tough and really smart. He seemed like a real intellectual, very conversant with history, and he had an intense seriousness of purpose. He certainly impressed me more than Bin Laden."

Abu Musab Al-Suri is today considered a key leader and strategist of the global jihadist movement, who has inspired much of ISIS' global campaign. His 1,500 page book *Call to Global Islamic Resistance* (Da'wat al-muqawamah al-islamiyyah al-'alamiyyah) has been described by acclaimed counter-terrorist expert Brynjar Lia as "the most significant written source in the strategic studies literature on Al-Qaeda." [186]

Lia also calls Al-Suri an 'architect' who 'through his writings has designed a comprehensive framework for future jihad'.

Abu Musab Al-Suri's book *'Call to Global Islamic Resistance'* is considered "the most significant written source in the strategic studies literature on Al-Qaeda." In this 2004 book issued on the Internet, Al-Suri promotes the theory of 'nizam, la tanzim' (system, without organization) with loose terror networks scattered around the world following a largely uniting ideology. [187]

Thus it states: "The main focus of military operations for resisting America and its allies now, must remain in the context of 'light gang warfare', 'urban terrorism', and the covert style, and especially in the context of solo operations and small and wholly separated resistance cells."[188]

The book formulates a strategy for the so-called jihadist movement and avers that its military theory should focus on two key tactics: 'solo or cellular jihad' that relates to individual jihadists (ideally less than 10 in number per unit) organizing and carrying out attacks with no connection or support from any jihadi group, and establishment of open jihadi fronts in regions of the world having conditions that are suitable for prolonged guerilla and urban warfare. Thus, these cells promote the 'jihadist movement' rather than any particular terrorist organization or leader.

He ranks the order of the preferred countries and regions to be targeted by terrorists and details ways of claiming responsibility of the attacks. He provides insights into how to identify the right targets and then how to attack them.[189]

According to Al-Suri, the 'mujahideen' should concentrate their energies on mainly five regions of the world: Afghanistan, Central Asia, Yemen Morocco and particularly Iraq. He asserts that the US occupation of Iraq has ushered in ' a historical new period' for global jihadist terror that was almost completely wiped out in Afghanistan after US operations post 9/11.

The final hundred pages of Al-Suri's book are devoted to references in the Hadeeth literature to Al-Qaeda's version of "apocalyptic jihad". It is one of the early instances of Salafi Jihadist thought playing up the so-called end-time prophecies in Islam to promote its version of jihad. The ISIS, more than Al-Qaeda, has subsequently developed this trend in violent Islamism which appears to be formally introduced by Al-Suri's book.

However, according to Jean-Pierre Filiu there is "nothing in the least rhetorical about this exercise (in Suri's book) in apocalyptic exegesis. It is meant instead as a guide for action."[190]

Al- Suri rakes up apocalyptic myth in his so-called treatise on Jihad, says Filiu, because "an appeal to the imminence of apocalypse would provide it (global Jihadist movement) with an instrument of recruitment, a framework for interpreting future developments, and a way of refashioning and consolidating its own identity. In combination, these things could have far-reaching and deadly consequences."[191]

ISIS has used many of the techniques detailed in this book during its terrorist operations in Iraq in recent years and is also employing the

Internet to create terror cells in various countries using some of Al-Suri's instructions.

b) Template for Terror: Abu Bakr Naji's 'Management of Savagery'

Author of atrocities: Influential Abu Bakr Naji, right, wrote the guide (left) that acts as a template for terrorism

Although Suri's treatise largely concentrates on techniques for conducting terrorist operations, the book that has most influenced ISIS' military operations in Iraq is said to be Abu Bakr Naji's *The Management of Savagery*[192] (*Idārat at-Tawahhush:Akhtar marhalah satamourrou biha l ummah*). Posted online in 2004 and circulated in Sunni Jihadi circles, the book provides an alternative to Suri's decentralized 'leaderless' approach by offering an "expansive plan for how a group of Muslim militants could violently seize land and establish their own self-governing Islamic state – much like the ISIS is doing today."[193] The book demonstrates patterns of "abominable savagery," which are witnessed in both the Islamic State and its earlier manifestations under Zarqawi.

Al-Naji calls on the so-called jihadists to carry out a merciless campaign to polarize populations and foment sectarian strife in order to create its own order out of the prevailing chaos. Thus, the book states: "The management of savagery can be defined very succinctly as the management of savage chaos!" "The increase in savagery is not the worst thing that can happen now or (as it has already happened) in the previous decade or those before it. Rather, the most abominable of the levels of savagery is less (abominable) than stability under the order of unbelief." Thus it states, "We must make this battle very violent, such that death is a heartbeat away, so that the two groups will realize that entering this battle will frequently lead to death."

According to William McCants, fellow at the Saban Center for Middle East Policy and director of the Project on U.S. Relations with the Islamic World at the Brookings Institution, who translated the book into English in 2006, "[The book] provides a roadmap for how to establish a caliphate," McCants adds[194]. "It lays out how to create small pockets of territorial control ... and how to move from there to a caliphate. It would not surprise me if the book were popular among the crew in Iraq [ISIS]."

Other analysts, such as Terrence McCoy of the *Washington Post*,[195] former MI-6 agent Alastair Crooke[196] and Lawrence Wright of *The New Yorker* also hold the view that this book is followed by the ISIS in its military strategy and operations. The book is itself testimony to the fact that terrorism, beheadings and savage acts – as perpetrated by the ISIS and other extremist Islamist groups since its publication – is not reflective of "whimsical, crazed fanaticism, but a very deliberate, considered strategy." According to Crooke, "The seemingly random violence has a precise purpose: It's aim is to strike huge fear; to break the psychology of a people — and according to reports this is exactly what [it] has succeeded in doing."[197]

According to Al-Naji, the killings are not just attempts to create terror, but are also meant to 'polarize' the population. The violence is intended to foment sectarian tensions and force sects to choose sides and "drag the masses into battle." Although ISIS literature never openly gives credit to Al-Naji's book for its tactics, its methods of creating chaos and large-scale violence ditto its style of operations and those of original founder, Abu Mu'sab Al-Zarqawi. The feature titled 'Hijarah to Khilafah', appearing in the first edition of the ISIS' slick magazine *Dabiq*, extols the indiscriminate violence of Zarqawi, including acts of provoking sectarian strife between Sunnis and Shiites:

> "Shaykh Abu Mus'ab (rahimahullah) implemented the strategy and required tactics to achieve the goal of Khilafah without hesitation. In short, he strived to create as much chaos as possible ... using attacks sometimes referred to as operations of "nikayah" (injury) that focus on causing the enemy death, injury, and damage.

> With chaos, he intended to prevent any taghut regime from ever

achieving a degree of stability that would enable it to reach a status quo similar to that existing in the Muslim lands ruled for decades by tawaghit. Such a status quo – consisting of powerful intelligence and security agencies – allowed the tawaghit to crush any Islamic movement that tried to only slightly raise its head and whisper its creed.

To achieve maximum chaos, the Shaykh focused on the most effective weapons in the arsenal of the mujahidin for Shaykh Abu Mus'ab (rahimahullah) creating chaos – vehicle bombs, IEDs, and Istishhadiyyin (martyrdom-seekers).

He would order to carry out nikayah operations dozens of times in a dozen areas daily, targeting and killing sometimes hundreds of apostates from the police forces and Rafidah. In addition to that, he tried to force every apostate group present in Iraq into an allout war with Ahlus-Sunnah (Sunnis). So he targeted the Iraqi apostate forces (army, police, and intelligence), the Rafidah (Shia markets, temples, and militias), and the Kurdish secularists (Barzani and Talabani partisans). In his speech titled "Hadha Bayanullin-Nasi wa li Yundharu Bih" (This Is a Declaration for the People That They May Be Warned by It), he threatened war on any Sunni tribe, party, or assembly that would support the crusaders.

Then when some so-called 'Islamists' entered into the democratic political process – ignoring what it entails of clearcut major 'shirk' (worshipping someone besides Allah) – he officially declared war on them in his speech titled 'Wa li Tastabina Sabilul-Mujrimin' (And Thus the Way of the Criminals Becomes Evident)."[198]

Later *Dabiq* states how after Al-Zarqawi, the leadership of the group practised the same methodology of creating widespread chaos and anarchy to eventually create the Khilafah.

c) Fouad Hussein's: 'Al-Zarqawi: Second Generation of Al-Qaeda'

In spite of widespread belief that Al-Qaeda's activities are random and do not follow any clear strategy, counterterrorism agencies have seized several documents over the years that point to Al-Qaeda's long term strategic plans and goals.[199]

One of the most important of these documents is derived from a book written by a radical Jordanian journalist Fouad Hussein, who according to Lawrence Wright "produced what is perhaps the most definitive outline of Al-Qaeda's master plan: a book titled *Al-Zarqawi: The Second Generation of Al-Qaeda*."[200]

Hussein claims that after having studied the failures of various Islamist movements, Al-Qaeda strategists have surmised that they lacked concrete and realistic goals. In response, the ideologues have drawn up a feasible plan within a well-defined timeframe, "covering the entire world". What is remarkable about this 2004 plan is that it has largely been able to meet most of its targets on schedule, such as deposing of Arab rulers in the 2010-13 timeframe and the establishment of the Caliphate in the fifth phase of the Plan covering the 2013-16 period.

The "Masterplan", as detailed in Hussein's book, was translated and commented upon in English by Yassin Musharbash in the German newspaper *Der Spiegel* on 12 August 2005.[201] It states that the 'insurgent network hopes to establish the Islamic Caliphate' in seven steps;

- **The first phase (2000 to 2003)** was characterised as the **'Awakening Phase'**. The aim in this phase was to provoke USA into declaring war on the Islamic world, thereby awakening the Muslims. 9/11 was a part of this strategy. Fouad writes that this phase began by striking the US ('the head of the serpent'), which caused the latter to "lose consciousness and act chaotically against those who attacked it. This also allowed the party that hit the serpent to lead the Islamic movement from the front."

- **The second phase (2003 to 2006)** has been dubbed by Al-Qaeda as the **'Eye-Opening Phase'**, whereby Muslims of the world would be made aware of "the Western conspiracy" against them. Al-Qaeda also believed that their organization would develop into a popular movement in this period.

- **The third phase (2007 to 2010)** is described as the **'Rising and Standing Up' Phase.** During this period there was to be increased focus on Syria and attacks on Israel.

- **The fourth phase (2010 to 2013)** covers the stage when insurgents would seek to bring down the hated Arab regimes. The resulting power vacuum would then strengthen the hands of the insurgents. It also states that Islamists would have started carrying out e-jihad by this time and would increase the use of gold as currency that would lead to bringing down the US dollar.

- **The fifth phase (2013 to 2016)** is the point when "Islamic Caliphate is declared". This has strangely come true with the establishment of the Caliphate in Iraq and Syria by ISIS. According to Hussein at this stage, the "Western fist in the Arab region" would have relaxed and "the international balance will change." Al-Qaeda and the Islamist movement will then attract powerful new economic allies, such as China, and Europe will fall into disunity.

- **The sixth phase from 2016 onward** will be a period of **'Total Confrontation.'** It will be characterized by the formation of the 'Islamic army,' which will instigate a "fight between believers and non-believers."

- **The seventh or the final phase** will be completed by 2020 and will lead to 'Definitive Victory' and the success of the Caliphate. According to Hussein, "The world will then realize the meaning of real terrorism." The victory will mean that "falsehood will come to an end. . . . The Islamic state will lead the human race once again to the shore of safety and the oasis of happiness."

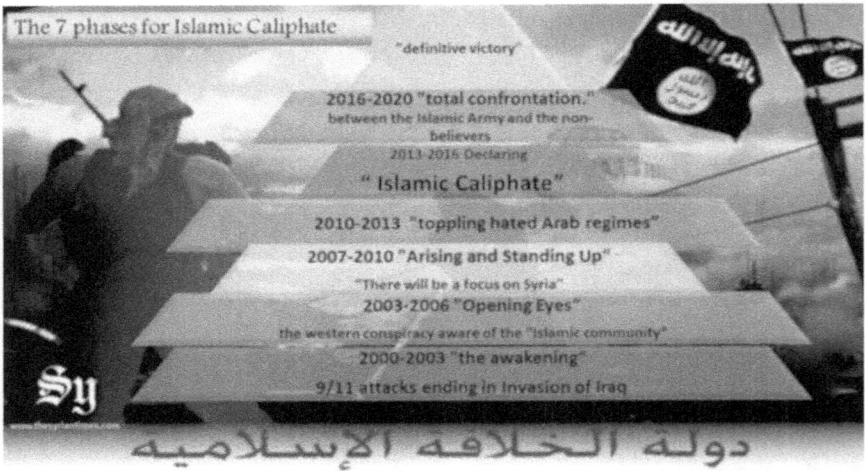

The 7 phases for Islamic Caliphate

"definitive victory"

2016-2020 "total confrontation."
between the Islamic Army and the non-believers

2013-2016 Declaring
" Islamic Caliphate"

2010-2013 "toppling hated Arab regimes"

2007-2010 "Arising and Standing Up"

"There will be a focus on Syria".
2003-2006 "Opening Eyes"

the western conspiracy aware of the "Islamic community"

2000-2003 "the awakening"

9/11 attacks ending in Invasion of Iraq

A graphic displaying the Al Qaeda-ISIS Seven Stage 'Masterplan' of Attaining Global Caliphate by 2020

The vision and strategies of these three treatises has deeply influenced ISIS warfare. If we are to believe the claims of Abu Musab Al-Suri, the "third generation of mujahideen" currently fighting in Iraq (after two earlier generations fought the Soviets and Americans in the 80s and 90s in Afghanistan) are getting trained in vicious urban warfare. This experience gained by the ISIS, will then be used by its foreign fighters on their return to their countries in the Middle East, Central Asia, the Philippines, Indonesia, Malaysia and European nations. Perhaps, if one were to combine this strategy with Hussein's sixth stage, it would usher in the period of 'Total Confrontation'. The 2020 plan detailed in Fouad's book is eerily similar to the five-year plan announced by the ISIS to form its Caliphate, which will include all Muslim-dominated territories in the world and beyond.

d) The Ba'athist Support to ISIS

Another influence in the structure, organization, warfare and even in the political objectives of the ISIS is that of Ba'athism, or that of ex-Ba'athists who joined the forces with the Islamic state between 2008 and 2010. In fact, the resurgence of the AQI after its near annihilation by the end of the last decade could be largely attributed to the inclusion of former Saddam military officials like Haji Bakr into the fold of ISIS, as highlighted in the earlier chapter. In its earlier form, Ba'athists sought to revive the glory of the Arab race by what it perceived as the gradual "corruption of its values and the legacy of colonialism".[202] Although Ba'athism was secular in outlook and separated religion from state, it still viewed Islam as symbol of the intellectual vitality of the Arab people.

Some Ba'athists joined the ISIS primarily to fight the Maliki government's anti-Sunni agenda, they were impressed in the way religious resistance resonated among Sunni masses of Iraq, even if it was of the Salafi/Takfeeri kind as opposed to the Ba'athist discourse. Thus, some ex-Baathists of Iraq have held elite positions in the ISIS hierarchy and have been masterminding its successes in the battlefield, thanks to their experience in the erstwhile Saddam army, and have compromised their ideological differences in order to protect and secure their Sunni identity. In fact, it is strange to see the Salafi leadership of the ISIS forging an 'unholy alliance' with the Sufi and Baathist groups such as Jaysh Rijal Al-Tariqa Al-Naqshbandiya (JRTN), in spite of their ideological animosity toward the secularists and Islamic mystics. However, differences between various factions of the Sunni Baathist groups in Iraq and the ISIS remain and the two have also reportedly confronted each other on occasions.

However, in spite of tensions JRTN leader and former Iraqi Vice President under Saddam, Izzat Ibrahim Al-Dourri is said to have hailed the leadership of the "heroes and knights of Al-Qaeda and the Islamic State" in an audio statement released on July 13.[203] Moreover, it has to be noted that IS appointed former Baathist general Azhar Al-Obeidi the governor of Mosul, shortly after capturing the city. They also made former Iraqi general Ahmed Abd-el Rashid the governor of Tikrit.[204]

In addition, both of Abu Bakr-Al-Baghdadi's deputies were former ranking officers in the Iraqi army. "Abu Ali Al-Anbari, the chief of Syria operations was a major general in (Saddam's) Iraqi Army and Fadl Ahmad Abdullah Al-Hayali (Abu Muslim Al-Turkmani), the chief of operations of Iraq was a lieutenant colonel in Iraqi military intelligence"[205] and former officer of the Iraqi special forces.[206] Moreover, according to information gathered from the safe-house of former ISIS General Military Council Leader Adnan Ismail Najem Bilawi in early June 2014, the ISIS had roughly a thousand: medium and top level field commanders, who all have technical, military and security experience."[207]

20.   The Five-Step Action Plan

The ISIS has charted its journey to statehood (in fact, its self-styled Caliphate or Khilafah) in five stages. These stages are described in the Arabic language as Hijrah (migration to the land of Shariah rule), Jamaah (Consolidation of Muslims of various nationalities and orientation as citizens of the state), Destabilizing Taghut (waging a bitter against the 'tyrants'), Tamkeen (Consolidation and Territorial Control)

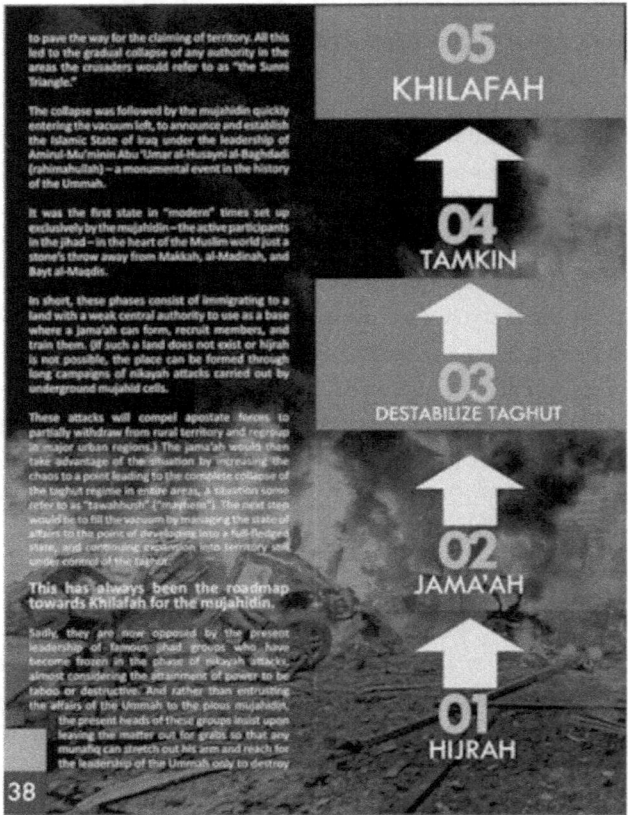

A page from the first issue of Dabiq illustrating the five step plan

and Khilafah (creation of Islamic Caliphate under ISIS' version of Shariah). Although for ISIS ideologues, the Khilafah as the quintessential Islamic State has been established, it still needs to spread to the rest of the Islamic world, if not to the whole world.

Therefore, it has to pass through the same stages as the seed state in order to complete its process of expansion. It is therefore important to understand what and how the ISIS seeks to achieve its goal of global Caliphate.

The ISIS has itself explained this five-step strategy in the very first edition of *Dabiq* (its online magazine, published for propaganda and recruitment).

a) *The Hijrah Stage (Call for Migration to ISIS' Territory):*

"The first priority is to perform hijrah from wherever you are to the Islamic State, from dārul-kufr (non-ISIS lands) to dārul-Islām... Rush to the shade of the Islamic State with your parents, siblings, spouses, and children. There are homes here for you and your families. *You can be a major contributor towards the liberation of Makkah, Madīnah, and al-Quds (Jerusalem).*"[208]

According to the ISIS propaganda, now that the Khilafah (or Caliphate) has been established it is incumbent upon every Muslim to leave the part of the world he or she lives in and migrate to the "Islamic State" as it is now religiously incumbent upon the person to do so.

The organization's mouthpiece *Dabiq* magazine states that earlier it was difficult for puritanical Muslims and jihadists to turn to a land where they could practice their faith in an Islamic system and environment, but now there are several options available to conduct jihad so that they could turn those regions into Islamic states. Thus, the *Dabiq* article states, "Al-hamdu lillah, there are now numerous more lands with conditions that support jihad, such as Yemen, Mali, Somalia, the Sinai Peninsula, Waziristan, Libya, Chechnya, and Nigeria, as well as parts of Tunis, Algeria, Indonesia, and the Philippines."[209] Boko Haram, six top leaders of the Tehreek-i-Taliban Pakistan led by Shahidullah Shahidm, dozens of jihadi leaders in Derna region of Libya, the Abu Sayyaf in the Philippines and Ansar Bayt al-Maqdis, the largest militant Islamic group in Egypt have sworn allegiance to the ISIS.

Therefore, the first edition of *Dabiq* urges jihadists from all over the world to migrate to these territories as well as to the so-called Islamic State, just as the jihadists following Abu Musab Al Zarqawi migrated to Afghanistan and then Iraq in their pursuit of establishing an Islamic state.

Referring to Abu Musab Al-Zarqawi, the founding father of the organization's ideology, *Dabiq* provides details of the strategy to call on people to do 'Hijrah' emigration. It is noteworthy that the ISIS is here employing the term of the Prophet's migration from Mecca to Madinah (known among Muslims as Hijrah) to their call for migration to the battlefields of jihad around the world, and principally to its own so-called 'Islamic State'.

The purpose of Hijrah according to the ISIS is to assemble (jamaah) Muslims in order to then build a prospective 'Khilafah'.

b) *The Stage of Jamaah (Gathering and Recruiting of Migrants)*

Once the 'Muslim' emigrants have been assembled in the proto-state (the stage called the Jamaah), they are then to be purified of their past patterns of behavior and thinking, as well as indoctrinated and trained in the ways of the organization. According to *Dabiq*, the Hijrah (emigration) would then lead to bay'ah (oath of allegiance), sam' (listening to the ISIS indoctrination), ta'ah (unswerving obedience to the leadership), and i'dad (training) for ribat and qital (fighting) in order to then attain shahadah (an embodiment of the ideal in life and death) and to attain Khilafah (the ideal of the Caliphate).[210]

Before new recruits and migrants arrive to areas of the so-called 'Islamic State' in Syria or Iraq, they have to secure tazkiyya (is a form of certification of being a 'pure soul' from an existing ISIS member living in their region. "After arriving recruits are brought to pre-arranged accommodations shared with other new members."[211]

During the several interviews that follow their personal information is logged, passports are copied and financial donations received. Thereafter, the new recruits have to undergo several weeks of religious and military training. The training involves the use of pistols, assault rifles, rocket propelled grenades and sometimes mortars. After being trained, the recruits are generally assigned to guard duty for several weeks before being assigned frontline military operations.[212]

The ISIS has put up several military camps in recent years, particularly under some of the major municipalities in their control.

c) *Stage of 'Nikayah' (Inflicting Injury) on Taghut (Tyrannical Adversary)*

The ISIS is brazen in admitting that it conducts a deliberate, brutal and methodical strategy to stoke sectarian conflicts, exploit Iraq's and Syria's political weakness, and inflict injury to the very fabric of society through a vicious military campaign in order to serve the interests of its so-called 'Islamic State'. It hails Al-Zarqawi's actions as in the words of its mouthpiece *Dabiq*, he strived to create as much chaos as possible ... (by) using attacks sometimes referred to as operations of 'nikayah' (injury) that focus on causing the enemy death, injury, and damage."[213]

In the following paragraph, it unabashedly adds: "With chaos, he

(Al-Zarqawi) intended to prevent any taghut (tyrant) regime from ever achieving a degree of stability that would enable it to reach a status quo similar to that existing in the Muslim lands ruled for decades ... [214] By conducting such seditious and terrorist campaigns, the so-called apostate forces were compelled to withdraw from rural territory to regroup the few major urban regions.

The *Dabiq* article then explains: "The jama'ah would then take advantage of the situation by increasing the chaos to a point leading to the complete collapse of the taghut (tyrant) regime in entire areas, a situation some refer to as 'tawahhush' ('mayhem').

The next step would be to fill the vacuum by managing the state of affairs to the point of developing into a full-fledged state, and continuing expansion into territory still under control of the taghut."

d) *Tamkin (Seizure of Territory and Consolidation) Stage*

After conducting a sustained terrorist/guerilla campaign of instability, the ISIS moves into the next gear of carrying out major military operations once it finds the opposition to have weakened substantially to put up a strong resistance and its aim from here is not just to weaken the opposition but to take advantage of the confusion and fill in the vacuum by seizing and controlling 'enemy' territory.

Thus the *Dabiq* states: "The next step (Tamkin) would be to fill the vacuum by managing the state of affairs to the point of developing into a full-fledged state, and continuing expansion into territory still under control of the taghut (tyrant)."

Thus, the lightning raid with which the ISIS suddenly gained control of Sunni territories around June 2014, [215] was not the result of a meek capitulation by Iraqi forces but the outcome of a long process of gradual attrition, following ISIS' multi-year offensive now dubbed as "Soldier's Harvest". In his US Congressional testimony of 2014, Brett McGurk noted, "the shattering of Iraqi security forces (ISF) is the result of years of patient preparatory operations. Early in Abu Bakr al-Baghdadi's tenure, the Islamic State of Iraq (ISI), the current group's forerunner, began targeting pro-government Arabs in a powerful multi-year campaign of assassinations that culminated in al-Baghdadi's 'Soldiers Harvest' campaign against on-duty and off-duty security force members from July 29, 2013, to June 2014."

This campaign not only conducted the demolition of soldier's homes, but a number of sophisticated close quarter assassination of troops manning checkpoints, and effective under vehicle improvised explosive device (IED) attacks on key officers and leaders. Although conducted throughout Iraq, the 'Soldier Harvest campaign was particularly focused on Mosul and Ninanwah province.

The campaign proved so effective that McGurk stated, "by day (Mosul city) would appear normal, but by night ISIS controlled the streets." Until the time came, when on June 6, 2014, the Iraqi Security Forces (ISF) became so brittle that they crumbled during three days of skirmishes in the city and fell in the hands of ISIS militants. [216]

Following the seizure of the territory, taking full control of its security and administrative affairs and integrating it with other parts of the so-called Islamic State is part of the consolidation process of 'Tamkin'. Therefore, the stages from Hijrah, Jamaah, Nikayah and Tamkin has always been the "roadmap to Khilafah for the mujahideen (i.e. jihadists). [217]

e) *The Khilafah Stage (The formation of the Islamic State)*

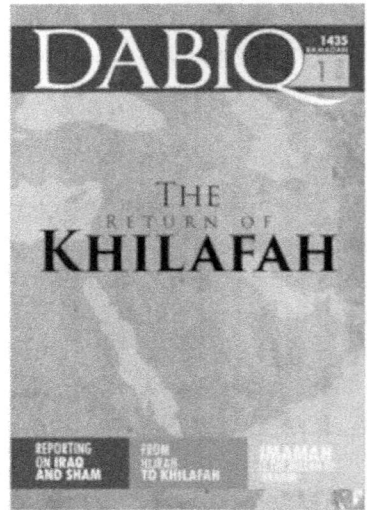

Cover page of the first issue of ISIS' online magazine *Dabiq*

As the ISIS consider its own version of Islam and its adherence to the faith as the only rightly guided way, it regards its own territory as the place where Islam is practiced in its pristine purity. Unlike other Muslim countries that follow either the medieval system of kingship or modern political systems like democracy, the ISIS champions itself as following the correct model of Islamic polity. To the ISIS, it is essentially the reinstatement of the Khilafah model of governance, as practised by the first four pious Caliphs (representatives of the Prophet). Therefore, it calls the Islamic State, the quintessential Khilafah, which it claims in time will grow to cover the entire Muslim world and go beyond. However, the germ of Khilafah has practically taken root under the so-called Islamic State and it wishes to repeat the same five stage strategy (or roadmap) listed above to physically expand itself.

The ISIS criticizes other jihadi groups in *Dabiq* to have not graduated from their anarchist mindset toward the goal of forming a Khilafah out of an allegedly misplaced sense of not falling prey to the corruption of power, as the ISIS has done.

Thus it states: "Sadly, they are now opposed by the present leadership of famous jihad groups who have become frozen in the phase of nikayah attacks, almost considering the attainment of power to be taboo or destructive." [218]

21. Fourth Generation Warfare (4GW)

In the words of former Senior Advisor to the United States Ambassador to Iraq and to the United States National Security Council Brett McGurk, the ISIS is "no longer a terrorist organization ... it is a full-blown army". [219]

Although its basic structure is that of a terrorist organization, it has proven capable of fighting as a light infantry force backed by heavy weapons and as a Maoist-style guerilla organization that in the words of former US Secretary of Defense Donald Rumsfeld is able to blend into the landscape.

In the words of Turkish military adviser Metin Gurcan: "Factors that boost tactical effectiveness of IS can be summarized as fluid and decentralized command and control structure; novel hybrid military tactics blending conventional warfare with terrorist tactics; effective use of armored platforms in offensive operations; dispersion; preservation of momentum at all costs; effective exploitation of topographic and human terrains; simplicity and flexibility in planning; and conducting operations and high levels of initiative and morale." [220]

This kind of warfare was presciently anticipated by several US war analysts in the late 1980s, particularly William Lynd, who feared that warfare would become increasingly decentralized in the future and would blur the lines between war and politics, combatants and civilians. They called this the fourth generation warfare (4GW) in which the major participants would be violent non-state actors. [221]

In fact, the ISIS to a great extent manifests all the facets of 4GW, in that it conducts hybrid warfare that combines conventional, irregular and cyberwarfare and unlike other contemporary armies of the world does not make sharp distinctions between strategic, operative and tactical levels. It hybridizes terrorist attacks, urban guerilla warfare and conventional warfare. For example, it is highly capable in deploying 10-men teams to carry out building-by-building, block-by-block clear and hold operations in urban terrain. It is also adept at conducting armor attacks at night and is skilled in accurate firing of their main tank guns with thermal cameras, and is capable of planting IEDs in critical areas and routes. [222]

Under the leadership of Abu Bakr Al-Baghdadi, the ISIS has developed its own style of command and control. During the 'Breaking the Walls' campaign (the name ISIS gave to its series of 24 major vehicle-borne improvised explosive device {VBIED} attacks and eight prison breaks from 2012 to 2013), the force repeatedly demonstrated its "recentralized" command and control system in 20 multi-city synchronized bombing waves. The last attack of this campaign was on July 21, 2013, when it breached the prison at Abu Ghraib and free 500 or more prisoners.

The strikes exemplify Al-Baghdadi's formula for "centralized control but decentralized execution" in that his command cell finalized the date of attacks but the regional (wilayat) commanders setting their level of participation as per local conditions. The executive orders of the

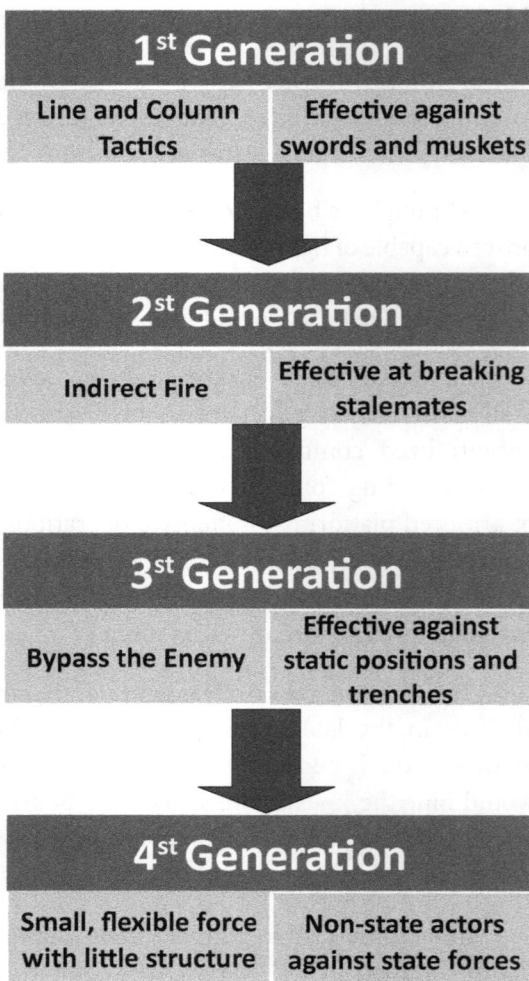

1st Generation	
Line and Column Tactics	Effective against swords and muskets

2st Generation	
Indirect Fire	Effective at breaking stalemates

3st Generation	
Bypass the Enemy	Effective against static positions and trenches

4st Generation	
Small, flexible force with little structure	Non-state actors against state forces

group are said to be brief, setting out what the mission is in the simplest of terms, leaving how it is to be carried out to field units.

This technique of launching multiple attacks on several axes helps the ISIS overwhelm the opponent's capacity to defend. "The group's capture of Jalula in Iraq on August 11, 2014 for example, involved the use of two large suicide car bombs followed by 12 separate suicide bombers, all of whom attacked separate checkpoints across the town on foot, opening routes for several coordinated ground assaults." [223]

Thus, ISIS has proven itself capable of "designing and implementing a multi-stage strategy aimed at engendering a chaotic power vacuum into which it can enter". [224]

The ability to surprise or shock on account of its mobility have been called the principal tactics of ISIS' offensive operations. It often achieves tactical surprise against the Iraqi and Kurdish forces through rapid approach marches that utilize Iraq's high quality road network and are carried out in night or dawn attacks. [225]

> Al-Baghdadi's formula for "centralized control but decentralized execution" has proven highly effective. The command cell finalizes the date of attacks but the regional commanders set their level of participation as per local conditions. The executive orders of the group are said to be brief, setting out what the mission is in the simplest of terms, leaving how it is to be carried out to field units.

"Probes and feints appear to be common elements in ISIL offensives, often apparently intended to test opposition, bypass solid defenses, and draw away enemy forces from the main target". [226].

According to Metin Gurcan, it is perhaps the first time that combat units (i.e. that of the ISIS) have made use of social media in military operations. According to him, "A typical ISIS operation goes like this: An ISIS armored unit of tanks or a mobile unit of eight to 12 fighters with two to three vehicles are informed by WhatsApp, a message on Facebook or Twitter or phone text message, and if this mode is not available through their own radio net, to assemble at a certain place at a certain time… Before its operations, ISIS disseminates propaganda messages via social media to enemy fighters and civilians living in the targeted urban settlements to demoralize and dishearten them. ISIS operations and logistics units that are thus alerted assemble at a meeting point within two to three hours, and after another hour and half of coordination discussions and logistics preparations the operation is underway." [227]

According to Iraqi military sources, "ISIS uses mortar shells and rocket-propelled grenades (RPGs) in combat operations, then pushes its fighters who are carrying these bombers and heavy machine guns – DShK 1938 (Dushka) – to reign down heavy fire on the enemy while its snipers hunt resisters at the height of the attack". [228].

Thus, the secret of many of ISIS' success has been attributed to the intensity of its firepower during its surprising and swiftness of attacks and its use of sniper fire from a marginal ploy to an important tactic of engagement during the peak of battle.

Thus, in almost all urban theatres in Iraq, ISIS' opponents have had to contend with three-pronged attack of sniper fires, IED mines and suicide bombers. Iraqi government forces are said to be trained in conventional warfare and are incapable of contending with this highly mobile and multi-pronged attack of ISIS forces.

On the other hand, the Peshmerga fighters have proven to be more capable in resisting ISIS' attacks in Kobane as they are also said to have extensively used sniper fire and suicide bombings in their fight against the ISIS. [229]

According to Iraq insurgency expert Ayman Al-Tamimi, whenever ISIS seizes a territory its forces quickly raise their banners over key administrative and security headquarters to create an impression on the opponents and resident population that they control the areas.

It then starts issuing basic instructions via leaflets, speakerphones and mosque speakers about its seizure. It surprisingly does not start implementing its version of Sharia law or religious police immediately after seizing control in order not to avoid an immediate local resistance. [230]

ISIS also behaves highly pragmatically when it comes to forging short-term "alliances of conveniences" with Sunni tribes and sects that do not fully follow its brand of extremist doctrines.

However, ISIS' offensive power has tended to diminish as it approaches majority Shi`a or Kurdish-populated areas, which has gradually started to undermine its image of invincibility and phenomenal expansion among its tribal supporters.

22. Maneuver Warfare of the Mongols

The former Grand Mufti of Egypt, Ali Gomaa has likened the ISIS to the 'Mongol Horde' of the 13th century. According to him, "When they (the ISIS) enter villages, they take the women and kill them. The Mongols did the same exact thing. Whenever they took over a city, they would kill the women. They would kill the children in front of their mothers.

"Then they would kill the men, and the rest would say: 'Enough. No one is left to protect us. Do as you wish. You are our masters now.'"[231]

However, the similarities with the legendary 'barbarian horde' do not end there. In the words of Gary Anderson, retired US Marine Corps colonel and civilian adviser in Iraq and Afghanistan, Baghdadi is adept at the maneuver warfare employed by the Mongol warriors of yore, which is part of Iraq's historic consciousness given Halagu's horrific sacking of Baghdad in 1258.

Thus he writes,[232] "Like the forces of Genghis Khan, al-Baghdadi's army consists of a small group of professionals … well versed in the theory and practice of maneuver warfare. Maneuver Warfare is not just about movement. It is about putting of all of your force's effects where they will do the most damage to the enemy."

> ಹ⦿ಚ
>
> **"Like the forces of Genghis Khan, Baghdadi's army consists of a small group of professionals, well versed in Maneuver Warfare. It gives more importance to mobility and swiftness. It is about putting your force's effects where they will do the most damage to the enemy."**
>
> ಹ⦿ಚ

Again, like the Mongols, ISIS gives more importance to mobility and swiftness and finds alternatives to overstretched lines of supply.

According to Keith Rozario[233]: "The Mongols could move their armies almost instantly, each Mongol soldier had more than just one horse, sometimes as many as five, and each of these horses carried supplies and they would ride together. The horses were always female for the soldiers to drink their milk, and their armies lived off the land.

"In this way, a moving Mongol force wouldn't need a supply line of caravans and ships (like those of the armies it met), but was self-sufficient and could move so quickly, many historians believe the Mongol numbers are greatly exaggerated because no one believed the speed of the Mongol army, that they assumed they were fighting two columns instead of one. ISIS may not ride on horses, but they use their modern equivalent–the Toyota Hilux. It moves faster than tanks and ISIS doesn't need a supply line either, when all they want they get from raided cities."[234]

23.   Terrorism as Military Tactics

Again, through the selective use of terror, the ISIS like the Mongols has been successful in gaining the upper hand against superior adversaries. "Iraqi government commanders in Baghdad found themselves issuing orders to subordinate leaders who have left the field. Junior soldiers woke up to see their commanders boarding mini-busses and panicked fearing the fate of fellow soldiers who had previously surrendered only to be massacred. This deliberate use of terror is selective as was the case with Genghis Khan. He massacred the populations of the first cities of any region that he attacked, and the word got around that resistance was futile. The great Khan conquered many cities, but based on his reputation, he had to lay siege to very few."

In this respect, ISIS is closer to the Mongols who used terrorism as a psy-ops and a propaganda tool. "The great Khan spread his propaganda message by rumor and fifth column plants disguised as merchants; Al-Baghdadi uses the social media and the web." On the one hand, the ISIS has used the gruesome beheadings and burnings of foreign civilians and soldiers to dare the US and its NATO allies to re-enter the Iraqi quagmire.

ISIS has also used such atrocities as a means to deter Arab allies of the global coalition from fighting the group and many of these countries at least temporarily suspended their military operations against the ISIS as a result.

According to Keith Rozario,[235] "The Mongols had a policy, surrender to them and you 'might' live, but put up a fight and you'll definitely die. It's a policy that serves to terrorize future cities more than it is about killing the sacked city. The ISIS uses the exact same tactic, every time they capture an Iraqi battalion, they line them up and start shooting them one by one — they then upload the images to Facebook to allow for their reputation to precede them. Iraqi forces, who are just 'fresh graduate' soldiers trembled at the terror and decide to flee, in much the same way as armies fled before the Mongols."

Unlike Al-Qaeda, the ISIS uses terrorism as a military strategy and not as an end in itself. In the words of William McCants, "The Islamic State stands apart from other [extremist] organizations. They are not bound by the structures of traditional Islamic warfare."

With its perverse form of warfare, the ISIS has transformed terrorism and the most heinous form of war crimes into a kind of mass communication in order to instill terror and panic among its opponents.

> *"The Islamic State (ISIS) stands apart from other [extremist] organizations. They are not bound by the structures of traditional Islamic warfare."*
>
> *- William McCants*

24. Human Rights Violations

Terrorism is also a perverse means of controlling a large civilian population. The United Nations Commission on Human Rights has stated that the ISIS, "seeks to subjugate civilians under its control and every aspect of their lives through terror." There have been many reports of the group's use of death threats, torture and mutilation to compel conversion to its brand of Islam and of Muslim clerics who refused to swear allegiance to the group. [236]

a) Large-Scale Religious, Sectarian and Ethnic Cleansing

ISIS brazenly directs its violence against Shia Muslims, indigenous Assyrian, Chaldean, Syriac and Armenian Christians, Yazidis, Druze, Shabak and Mandeans. Amnesty International has provided details of how the group has "systematically targeted non-Arab and non-Sunni Muslim communities, killing and abducting hundreds, possibly thousands, and forcing more than 830,000 others to flee the areas it has captured since 10 June, 2014."[37]

The ISIS has also been accused by the UN for committing "mass atrocities" and "war crimes" for the mass killing of 250 Syrian Army soldiers near Tabqa Air base.[238] Another reported killing of military prisoners has been reported in Camp Speicher, where a thousand to 1,700 Iraqi army soldiers are said to have been shot. The ISIS has also been the ancient cultural and religious heritage of Iraq. In the words of Saad Eskander, the head of Iraq's National Archive, "For the first time you have cultural cleansing... For the Yazidis, religion is oral, nothing is written. By destroying their places of worship … you are killing cultural memory. It is the same with the Christians – it really is a threat beyond belief"[239].

b) Atrocities Against Women and Children

The group has executed civilians (men and women) on charges of adultery, homosexuality, watching pornography, rape, blasphemy, murder and for renouncing Islam. These executions have been carried out in various forms ranging from stoning to death, crucifixions, beheadings and throwing people off tall buildings.[240] Again, the UN is now looking into claims that the ISIS may be harvesting organs from slain civilians and gaining financial benefits by trafficking the body parts to European black markets.[241]

The group has recruited children as young as nine as policemen and have given them guns to patrol the streets of Mosul and make arrests. They are called 'Cubs of the Caliphate'. On March 11, 2015, the group released a video showing a boy of around 12 years of age executing for the ISIS a 19-year-old "Israeli spy" by shooting at the kneeling man's head.[242] Another video released in January 2015, showed a boy executing two Russian spies.[243]

There have also been many incidents of sexual abuse and enslavement of women and girls in ISIS-controlled areas, particularly against females

The beheading of Kurdish woman soldier, known as Rehana, by ISIS fighters shocked the world

of Christian and Yazidi communities. According to Haleh Esfandiari, Director of the Middle East Program at the Woodrow Wilson International Center for Scholars, ISIS fighters invariably abuse local women once they capture an area. "They usually take the older women to a makeshift slave market and try to sell them. The younger girls ... are raped or married off to fighters." She adds, "It's based on temporary marriages, and once these fighters have had sex with these young girls, they just pass them on to other fighters."[244]

British author and human rights activist Nazand Begikhani has collected information about the criminal behavior of ISIS fighters against women of Yazidi communities. She states: "These women have been treated like cattle... They have been subjected to physical and sexual violence, including systematic rape and sex slavery. They've been exposed in markets in Mosul and in Raqqa, Syria, carrying price tags."[245] It has also been reported that young Yazidi girls raped by ISIS fighters committed suicide by jumping to their death from Mount Sinjar.[246] In mid-October, the UN confirmed that 5,000-7,000 Yazidi women and children were abducted by ISIS and sold into slavery.[247] In fact, ISIS has openly accepted and given religious justification for its practice of enslaving and selling

Yazidi women.[248]

In a perverse interpretation, the *Dabiq* purportedly cites a Hadeeth which predicts the revival of women's slavery by the end of the world. Thereafter, the digital magazine claims that as the world is fast approaching its end it is natural that the evil practice be revived.[249] Many Muslim scholars from around the world have condemned the reintroduction of the ancient practice of slavery and sex with captured women as un-Islamic and have said that ISIS' fatwas are invalid due to their inconsistencies with Islamic law.[250]

In late May 2015, ISIS captured the historical city of Palmyra and reportedly slaughtered over 400 people there, mostly women and children. According to Syrian state news agency: "The terrorists have killed more than 400 people.. and mutilated their bodies, under the pretext that they cooperated with the government and did not follow orders."

c) Beheadings and Burnings

But perhaps the most gruesome of crimes the ISIS has conducted with the deliberate intent of causing terror among its opponents and people worldwide have been the large number of beheadings and burnings of hostages conducted since 2014. Not only has the ISIS beheaded a number of people from various countries, but it has posted the videos of these executions on various social media. On July 25, 2014, the photographs of the beheadings of a number of Syrian soldiers were posted on social media. According to news reports, ISIS beheaded as many as 75 Syrian soldiers in the city of Raqqa. Last year, an Australian citizen Khaled Sharrouf, who migrated and joined the ISIS ranks, posted the picture of his seven-year-old son holding the decapitated head of a Syrian soldier.

Then around August 19, 2014, the infamous ISIS executioner 'Jihadi John' carried out his first beheading of US photojournalist James Wright Foley. The release of the beheading video by the ISIS on social media drew global condemnation. 'Jihadi John and 'Jailer John' are the pseudonyms given by the hostages held by the executioner, who is allegedly a British national belonging to a terror cell calling itself 'The Beatles'. The pseudonym is a reference to John Lennon of the Beatles, and other members of the cell are 'George,' 'Paul' and 'Ringo' after the names of the other pop stars of the legendary band. In February 2015, British officials claimed to have identified

'JIHADI JOHN'

The infamous 'Jihadi John' is a person shown in several videos produced by ISIS carrying out beaheadings of a number of hostages in 2014-15. On February 26, 2015, The Washington Post identified the 'beheader' as Mohammed Emwazi, a 26-year-old British citizen (born 17 August, 1988). A group of hostages had nicknamed the beheader as 'Jihadi John', for he was part of a four-person terrorist cell with British accents whom they called 'The Beatles'. (Picture of Mohammed Emwazi)

Jiadi John as Mohammed Emwazi, a Kuwaiti-born Londoner, who had traveled to Syria in 2012 and joined the ISIS there.[251] The gruesome video was soon followed by pictures of decapitation of Lebanese Army Sergeant Ali al-Sayyed on August 28, 2014. The pictures of his beheading were posted on Twitter by an ISIS member, Abu Musaab Hafid Al-Baghdadi.

Thereafter, 'Jihadi John' was seen conducting the beheading of Steven Sotloff, a US journalist for the *Time* magazine, in a video released on September 2, 2014. Sotloff had been kidnapped in Aleppo, Syria, in 2013 and held captive by ISIS militants. David Haines, a humanitarian aid worker from the group Agency for Technical Cooperation and Development who was assessing the Atmeh refugee camp near the Turkish border was abducted by ISIS in March 2013. Haines beheading video, titled 'A Message to the Allies of America', which showed it being conducted by 'Jihadi John' was released by ISIS on September 13, 2014. Lebanese Army soldier Abbas Medlej, Hervé Gourdel (a French citizen held by ISIS affiliated in Algeria), British humanitarian worker Alan Henning and Peter

Edward Kassig (whom in captivity became Muslim and took the name Abdul-Rahman Kassig) were all beheaded by the ISIS between September to November 2014. In addition, the ISIS has beheaded several Syrian, Kurdish and Egyptian nationals.

In December 2014, after suffering some military setbacks, ISIS reportedly beheaded about 100 foreign fighters of its own force on charges of desertion. Then in January 2015, ISIS gave the Japanese government a 72-hour deadline for the release of two Japanese hostages in its custody for a ransom of US $200 million. When the deadline passed without the payment of ransom, the ISIS released the beheading video of Haruna Yukawa. The deadline passed without fulfillment of the ransom, and a video of Yukawa's beheading was released. Later in the same month, the group released another video apparently showing the decapitation of Goto Jogo by the so-called Jihadi John. In the video, "A Message to the Government of Japan," Jihadi John apparently addressed Japanese prime minister Shinzo Abe and held him responsible for the killing by claiming "because of your reckless decision to take part in an unwinnable war, this knife will not only slaughter Kenji, but will also carry on and cause carnage wherever your people are found. So let the nightmare for Japan begin."

These beheadings triggered a new wave of shock and revulsion around the world at the barbarity of the ISIS. A grim-faced Abe could hardly contain his grief and annoyance in brief remarks to reporters: "I feel strong indignation at this inhumane and contemptible act of terrorism … I will never forgive these terrorists." Turning the savagery even more gruesome, ISIS posted a video on its Al-Hayat Media Center, 'Message signed in blood to the Nation of the Cross'. In the video, the beheadings of 21 Coptic Egyptian masons was shown being carried out on the sea shore in Libyan city of Tripoli.

According to Professor Ibrahim al-Marashi, ISIS's earlier incarnations used beheadings to force foreign policy changes such as getting countries such as the Philippines to withdraw from the Iraq War. Now, ISIS is using beheadings of locals to intimidate people, including their own soldiers, into obeying the dictates of a weak state. Beheadings of Westerners are designed to strike back at the United Kingdom and the United States for military actions against ISIS that they have no other way of responding to. "With an act of a sword, they manage to force both [American President] Obama and [British Prime Minister] Cameron to react. The two men, who control the world's most advanced militaries, find themselves at the mercy of the sword. Both displayed physical pain and grief when they condemned the way their nationals died." says al-Marashi.

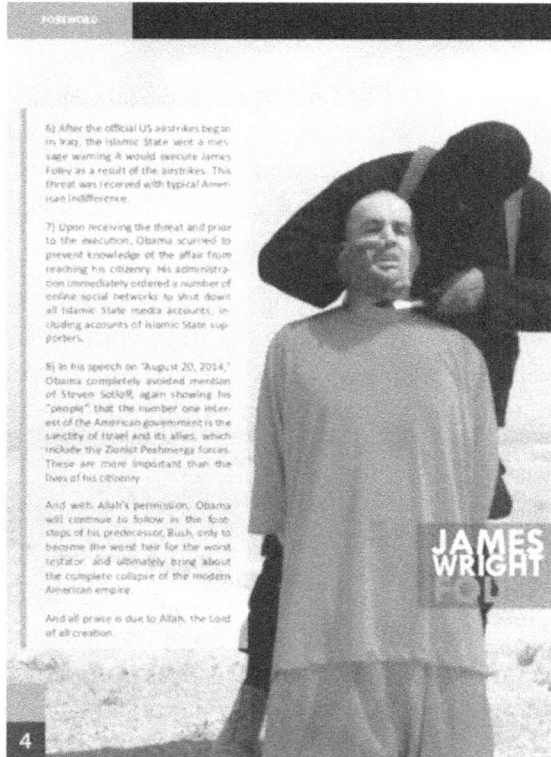

"Terror marketing" to recruit new fighters seems another motivation. "Some of these men have sort of a pornographic attraction to these violent scenes, these violent beheading videos. It really sort of energizes them." said Paul Cruickshank, a terrorism analyst for CNN.

Meanwhile, ISIS is said to have beheaded two groups of prisoners, believed to be Ethiopian Christians.[252] The group produced a video showing the two groups of men, one in orange jumpsuit and the other in black, being killed in different locations in Syria.

In addition to beheadings, the ISIS has also resorted to burning hostages to death, particularly Muslims.

On February 3, 2015, the ISIS released the video of Jordanian pilot Muath Al-Kassabeh being burned to death while trapped in a cage. Al-Kassabeh was a hostage of the ISIS after his F-16 fighter aircraft crashed near Raqqah in Syria on 24 December 2014.

The video was released after the Jordanian government had asked the ISIS for proof of the pilot being alive in its custody before exchanging him with a woman sentenced to death by Jordan (Sajida Al-Rishawi) for attempting terrorism and possessing explosives.

The ISIS justified burning the Jordanian pilot by claiming that it was a punishment that befitted a Murtadd (a Muslim renegade) on the basis of Qisas (retribution), for he had committed the crime of hurling fire down the ISIS territories from his fighter jet.

However, in its justification for the heinous act, *Dabiq* remarkably mentioned the Hadith which mentions that the Prophet has instructed against punishing people with fire; in its own words: "the authentic statement of Allah's messenger (sallallāhu 'alayhi wa sallam), "None should punish with fire except Allah" [Sahīh al-Bukhārī]".

In addition to the burning of the Jordanian pilot, there were reports that ISIS had burned to death at least 45 people in the Iraqi town of Al-Baghdadi, according to local police. In addition to the burning of the Jordanian pilot, there were reports that ISIS had burned to death at least 45 people in the Iraqi town of Al-Baghdadi, according to local police.

"Exactly who these people were and why they were killed is not clear, but Colonel Qasim al-Obeidi said he believed some were members of the security forces," the BBC reported in mid-February of 2015.

The large-scale atrocities carried out by the ISIS and other extremist groups in Syria and Iraq have worsened the already difficult humanitarian situation in the two countries, following the Syrian civil war of 2011.

It has been reported that almost four million people have fled abroad to escape the fighting in Syria since 2011.[253]

Most have gone to Lebanon and Turkey - but a significant number have also gone to Iraq.

Syrian refugees have put pressure on local services and infrastructure in Iraq - which is also having to cope with the return of many Iraqi refugees from Syria.

In addition, the UN estimates there are more than 2 million Iraqis who have been forced to leave their homes to escape the conflict and are displaced within the country or elsewhere.[254]

25. ISIS and the WMDs

Meanwhile, there have been allegations that the ISIS has used low-intensity chemical attacks during at least one of its military operations. Kurdish authorities in Iraq said in early March 2015 that they had evidence that ISIS had used chlorine gas as a chemical weapon against peshmerga fighters.[255]

The allegation by the Kurdistan Region Security Council, is in reference to a 23 January suicide truck bomb attack in northern Iraq. Earlier, Iraqi officials have made similar allegations about the militants using the low-grade chemical weapons against them.

There has also been alarm over the ISIS' stated intention of trying to buy a nuclear bomb "through weapons dealers with links to corrupt officials" in Pakistan and detonate it in the US, as stated by the ISIS' hostage journalist John Cantlie in an article titled "The Perfect Storm", which has appeared in its online propaganda magazine *Dabiq* (Issue 9).

Drawing the horrifying scenario, Cantlie writes: "Let me throw a hypothetical operation onto the table. The Islamic State has billions of dollars in the bank, so they call on their wilayah in Pakistan to purchase a nuclear device through weapons dealers with links to corrupt officials in the region. The weapon is then transported overland until it makes it to Libya, where the mujahidin move it south to Nigeria. Drug shipments from Columbia bound for Europe pass through West Africa, so moving other types of contraband from East to West is just as possible. The nuke and accompanying mujahidin arrive on the shorelines of South America and are transported through the porous borders of Central America before arriving in Mexico and up to the border with the United States. From there it's just a quick hop through a smuggling tunnel and hey presto, they're mingling with another 12 million "illegal" aliens in America with a nuclear bomb in the trunk of their car."[256]

Although the British photojournalist writing for the ISIS that such a scenario may appear far-fetched, he calls it, "the sum of all fears for Western intelligence agencies and it's infinitely more possible today than it was just one year ago. And if not a nuke, what about a few thousand tons of ammonium nitrate explosive?"

The passage then warns ominously: "They'll be looking to do something big, something that would make any past operation look like a squirrel shoot, and the more groups that pledge allegiance the more possible it becomes to pull off something truly epic."

The links of some factions of the Takreek-i-Taliban (TTP) of Pakistan with the ISIS and the open assertion by the ISIS that they intend to acquire a nuclear weapon soon should raise alarm bells around the world even if such prospects might appear remote at present.

It has to be noted that after the capture of Mosul by the ISIS 88 pounds of uranium from Mosul University went missing. The ISIS then claimed on Twitter in December 2014 that they had the 'dirty bomb' and had 'terror' plans for London.[257]

26.   Weaknesses in Warfare and Recent Reversals

The ISIS has suffered many setbacks and reversals on the battlefield in 2015. According to a US assessment, Kurdish and Iraqi forces have reclaimed more than 25 percent of ISIS-held territories inside Iraq. At its peak, ISIS was in control of 55,000 square kilometers in northern and western Iraq, but the recaptured areas have pushed ISIS back from an area between 4,100 and 5,200 square miles or 11,000 and 13,500 square kilometers.[258]

The success in reclaiming the strategically important city of Tikrit[259] and the Syrian-Turkish border city of Kobane by Kurdish Peshmerga forces has been seen as a turning point in the fight against ISIS. These successes have exposed some chinks in the ISIS armor and have unraveled the myth of ISIS' invincibility among its supporters. However, the recent capture of the city of Ramadi and the ancient city of Palmyra has emphasized that the threat of ISIS is not on the wane. Still, some weaknesses in its strategy and warfare are becoming apparent.

a) *Overreach*: The ISIS is fighting on multiple fronts in Iraq and Syria. In the month of March 2015 alone, Iraqi military and Shiite militias (principally led by the fighters belonging to Moqtada Al-Sadr) have sent forces to fight with ISIS fighters in Tikrit, Samarra, Kirkuk, Mosul.[260] ISIS forces seem overstretched and there is clear possibility of them being hemmed in from various sides in the coming months.

b) *Infamy for Extreme Violence*: The ISIS has only been successful in running over Sunni-dominated regions in Iraq and Syria. There is great hostility toward the movement in areas having non-Sunni populations. The ISIS' own propaganda campaign of conducting gory beheadings and public burnings (particularly of the captured Jordanian pilot) has made it unpopular even among Sunni populations in Jordan, and the Gulf Arab states.

c) *Exclusion from the Jihadist Bandwagon*: The ISIS has put itself into a corner by openly criticizing many Jihadi organizations like Al-Qaeda and calling many prominent Muslim leaders, like Hamas leader Ismail Haniyeh and former Egyptian leader Mohammed Mursi hypocrites. There is no major Islamic or jihadi organization that supports the group today, with the exception of the upstart Boko Haram in Nigeria and factions of the Tehreek-e-Taliban in Pakistan. Even extremist ideologues like Abu Muhammad Al-Maqdisi (the mentor of ISIS' founding father) and Abu Qatada Al-Filistini have been outspoken in their condemnation of ISIS and its horrible atrocities.

d) *Poor Muslim Response to the Caliphate Claim*: By declaring the Islamic State as the Caliphate, the ISIS thought it could trump all other jihadist organizations by realizing their coveted dream, but has in the process only isolated itself from the Muslim mainstream and caused more acrimony and hatred towards it in the process. Virtually unknown within the global jihadist community until recently, it was presumptuous on the part of Abu Bakr Al-Baghdadi to call on the entire Muslim world to acknowledge him as its Caliph and to declare that whoever does not recognize him as such is an apostate. In this instance, the only claim to legitimacy would have been its success in gaining important Muslim territory, which the ISIS has been unable to gain since about September of 2014.

e) *The Diminishing of Funds*: With the ongoing aerial bombing of oil wells and installations, the ISIS is reportedly losing one of its most important sources of revenue. Other forms of funding are also drying up as most of the hostages have been beheaded in the absence of the payment of ransom money. *The Economist* reports that the ISIS may have lost upto 75 percent of its revenues by March 2015.[261] This has made it harder to run its military operations and provide administrative services to the 8 million people under its charge.

f) *Large Number of Desertions Among ISIS Fighters:* There are increasing reports of internal tensions within ISIS ranks. Residents complain of extortion, violent repression and decline in public services.[262] The group has started to kill its own soldiers, sometimes for running away from battle and at least in one instance for beheading people without receiving any orders from the leadership.

g) *Discrimination Between Local and Foreign Fighters:* Another big challenge facing the ISIS is the apparent unraveling of the so-called Caliphate's promise of equality among its local and foreign followers and the visible difference in treatment between the two. For one, foreigners in the organization earn as much as twice more than local fighters. Foreign fighters also receive far better living accommodations in ISIS-controlled cities and are less frequently deployed to the front line than their Syrian or Iraqi counterparts.

This discrimination is said to have festered resentment among ISIS forces, which has been visible in the war theatres of Tikrit and Kobane. "The key challenge facing ISIS right now is more internal than external," Lina Khatib, the director of the Carnegie Middle East Center in Beirut, recently told The Washington Post. "We're seeing basically a failure of the central tenet of ISIS ideology, which is to unify people of different origins under the caliphate. This is not working on the ground. It is making them less effective in governing and less effective in military operations."[263]

Chapter Five
Metastasizing Monstrosity and Global Response

Blood is seen in the Mediterranean Sea in a video that recorded the beheading of hostages by ISIS supporters in Libya in February. In the video, the jihadis said they now planned to 'conquer Rome'

"As the territory of the Islamic State crosses from one border to another like a wildfire that is burning out of control, it'll be only a matter of time before the Islamic State reaches the Western world."

'The Perfect Storm', Dabiq, Issue 9

27.   ISIS Global: The Cyber Caliphate

In less than a year, since its capture of Mosul, the ISIS has spread its tentacles in over a dozen countries, with several terrorist groups swearing allegiance to Caliph Ibrahim across the globe. Thus, the ISIS has gone global and perhaps the most important contributor to this success has been its adroit use of Internet, more particularly the social media and 'Dark Web'.

The ISIS has a sophisticated and effective communications strategy that employs online media tools to disseminate its propaganda and for recruiting members worldwide.

It is also known to have carried out several cyber attacks, so far against Western websites, such as the Dublin Rape Crisis Centre in Ireland, the Southwest Montana Community Federal Credit Union in the US, Third Street Brewhouse, and the Montauk Manor.[264]

It is also claimed that people claiming to be sympathetic to ISIS hacked the Twitter and Youtube accounts for the US military command that oversees operations in the Middle East (CentCom) even though Pentagon stated: "operational military networks were not compromised and there was no operational impact."[265]

Although Osama bin Laden was the first terrorist to use Internet technology in 1997, the ISIS has raised 'cyber jihad' to a whole new level. Starting off from static websites, it moved on to developing chat forums, publishing online magazines and now making innovative uses of today's highly fast and interactive social media platforms.

According to a Geneva Center for Security Policy (GCSP) paper in 2015, the ISIS is an "active user of blogs, instant messaging, video sharing sites, Twitter, Facebook, Instagram, WhatsApp, Tumbler and AskFM"[266]

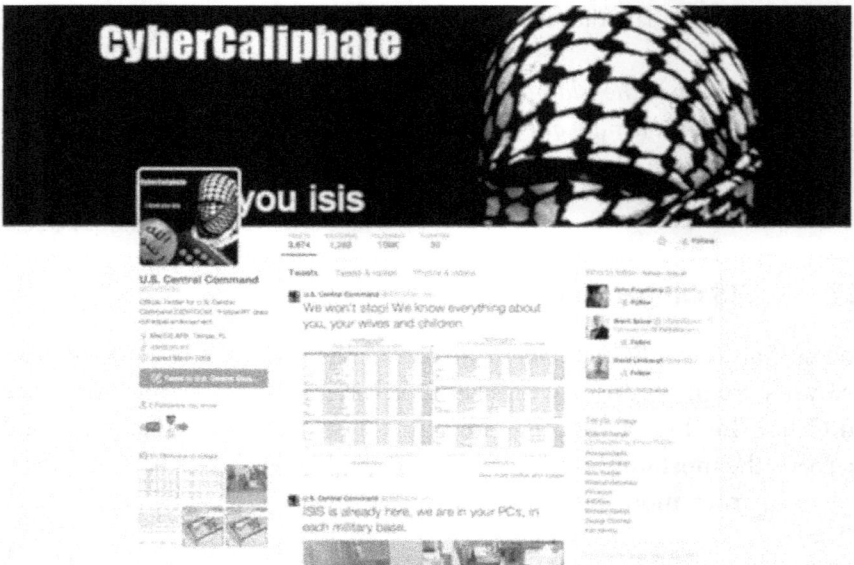

The GCSP study claims that the ISIS media campaign is supervised by a Syrian born in Saudi Arabia named Abu Amr Al Shami, who was earlier the leader of Aleppo. The ISIS produces and online magazine called *Dabiq*, which has so far published eight issues.

First published in June 2014, the magazine is published in Englsih, Arabic, French, German and Russian. Surprisingly, the ISIS does not publish literature in non-Arabic languages spoken in Muslim countries like Turkish, Persian, Urdu, Hausa, Pashto etc. This clearly illustrates its revulsion to any language spoken by Muslims other than Arabic.

The Al-Hayat Media Center is the ISIS wing for producing video content. In July 2014, it released 11 films in English, which were shot in high definition, with crisp editing and proficient branding techniques.[267]

Before ISIS launched its attack on Moul, it released a film called "The Clanging of the Swords IV" with slow motion graphics and aerial drone footage. This is said to have been useful in demoralizing Iraqi soldiers before the raids began.

The ISIS recently set up a new media wing to lure women, which is called the Zora Foundation that posts videos and tweets online and has gained over 3,200 followers. The so-called UMM network employs Twitter to attract women to their websites, which are filled with ideological messages and to seduce them to get married to jihadis. The supposed "good life" in the Caliphate is highlighted among pictures of kittens, desire wear and children wearing football jerseys.

However, Al-Furqan

> **"Slick propaganda through social media that goes like this: 'Troubled soul, come to the Caliphate, you will live a life of glory, these are the apocalyptic end times, you will find a life of meaning here fighting for our so-called Caliphate and if you can't come, kill somebody where you are.' That is a message that goes out to troubled souls everywhere,"**
>
> **Director of FBI James Comey**

105

remains the "official" media wing of the ISIS, which posts messages from the leadership. While, chat forums and discussion portals were widely used in early 2000, the ISIS and other terrorist groups have made their presence felt in the Dark Internet, where only hard to find websites and secretive networks, not accessible to search engines exist. To access these forums strict codes of membership, authentication and passwords are required.

ISIS distinguishes itself from other terrorist networks in that it freely uses hashtags like "#AllEyesonISIS", and most recently "CalamityWillBefallUS". According to the GCPS study, ISIS uses "twitter bombs" which redirect trending hashtags to Twitter websites and other material related to the terror group. "In the fall of 2014, there were at least 45,000 Twitter accounts used by IS supporters, 73 percent had an average of 500 supporters, others had upto 50,000 followers."[268]

India had its own ISIS Twitter handler in Mahdi Masroor Biswas, a 24-year-old management executive in an multi-national company, who worked as an ISIS propaganda activist, tweeting and retweeting thousands of messages. He is alleged to have interacted with key ISIS figures and with UK-based jihadists and is said to have 17,700 followers on his Twitter account and received about two million hits a month. The court remanded him for 15 days in police custody for investigation.[269]

One of the reasons behind the success of the ISIS in luring a large number of Muslims to their extremist organization is that many young Muslims suffer from a profound identity crisis unlike any experienced in modern Islamic history. According to Farah Pandith -, a former Special Representative to Muslim Communities at the US Department of State, who has conducted extensive research on the subject – argues that since 9/11, young Muslims have suffered intense scrutiny because of their religion. Earlier, a close-knit family circle within a larger community could offer a response. In today's insular communities, young Muslims are increasingly turning to the Internet for answers and are being misguided by some of the extremist messages offered online.

The ISIS message is getting particularly favorable response from impressionable young men in prisons, ghettos and refugee camps in Afghanistan, Bosnia, Chechnya, Iraq, Libya and Syria.

The angry and disgruntled youth of the Arab Spring across the Middle

East and Europe also provide a receptive target audience for the ISIS cyber jihad campaign.

28.   Growing Influence in Arabian Peninsula

In late April, the ISIS released a video showing 20 men wearing desert camouflage uniforms carrying out carefully choreographed rifle drill. The video stated that the group is part of the ISIS Caliphate in Yemen.[270]

This ISIS group has named itself as 'Soldiers of the Caliphate in Yemen' and some analysts believe that their aim is to take over Al-Qaeda in the Arabian Peninsula (AQAP), which has strongholds in the south and south-east of Yemen.

In March 2015, this group is said to have conducted a series of coordinated suicide bomb attacks at two mosques in Houthi-held territories in Sanaa. It is reported that four bombers, wearing explosive belts targeted worshippers in and around the crowded mosques during Friday prayers killing 137 people and wounding 357.

Then on May 23, 2015, ISIS claimed responsibility for a suicide bombing in a Shiite mosque in Saudi Arabian in the village of Qudayh. A total of 21 worshippers were reportedly killed in the attack and 81 were injured.[271]

A still from the video released by the ISIS-affiliated group in Yemen.

Again in late April, Saudi Arabia arrested 93 suspected ISIS members for trying to plot several terrorist attacks in the country. One of their alleged plan was to bomb the US embassy with a car bomb.[272]

The Saudi Interior Ministry also revealed that the accused were in the process of recruiting and training new members, were testing explosives and acquiring firearms, as well as plotting to attack security facilities and residential areas.

The government also announced that a recent killing of two Saudi policeman was carried out by the ISIS. It is to be noted that the ISIS leadership has called upon its supporters to mount attacks inside Saudi Arabia.

29. 'First Drops of Rain' in Africa

In fact, the eighth issue of the ISIS' mouthpiece '*Dabiq*,' focuses exclusively on the rise of the group's influence in the continent of Africa. The cover page is titled 'Shariah Alone Will Rule Africa' and states that its presence is expanding in Libya, Tunisia, Algeria, The Sinai Peninsula and West Africa.

Boko Haram leader Abubakar Shekau pledged allegiance to the ISIS leader Abu Bakr Al-Baghdadi in March 2015

ISIS has released a new issue of its recruitment magazine which is focused solely on expanding its presence across Africa, as the terror group's propaganda strategy continues to develop.

The magazine shows ISIS spokesman Muhammad al-Adnani congratulating the Nigerian radical group Boko Haram for "joining the caravan" of jihad, saying that they would "now guard yet another frontier of the Khilafah [caliphate]". In early March 2015, Boko Haram pledged allegiance to ISIS in an online message, which was then accepted by the so-called Islamic State. The African terrorist group has been fighting a six-year insurgency against Nigerian authorities to establish an Islamic "caliphate".

The magazine also speaks of ISIS's growing influence in Libya and Syria. The organization has managed to raise three affiliate groups in Libya, namely ISIS Tripoli (West), ISIS Barqa (East) and ISIS Fezzan (South). By exploiting the security vacuum in the country, the ISIS has seized control of the coastal town of Derna and controls key buildings in the central city of Sirte.[273] It has also carried out a series of attacks against targets in the Libyan capital, Tripoli. The ISIS has also called on its Libyan "soldiers" to wage war against the... the House of Representatives and the General National Congress", the two bodies which form Libya's internationally-recognised government in the country's eastern city of Tobruk.

Recently, the Tunisian government had expressed concerns over the return of its citizens from ISIS-held territories in Iraq and Syria as fully-trained jihadists. In figures released by the UK-based International Centre for the Study of Radicalisation and Political Violence (ICSR) earlier this year, it was revealed that up to 3,000 Tunisians had travelled to Syria and Iraq to join the ranks of radical extremist groups, the highest of any country in the world.

Thereafter, ISIS claimed responsibility for a raid on Tunisian national museum, in which two gunmen shot dead 20 foreign tourists. ISIS called the attack as the "first drop of rain."

30.   US and Europe: ISIS Claims 'Countdown to Terror'

The ISIS has spread its influence in almost all parts of the Western hemisphere, particularly in the US, where FBI Director James Comey says it has woven "a chaotic spider web", with young Muslim men being radicalized in all 50 states. The menace of ISIS infestation is particularly severe in the states of Illinois, Indiana, Wisconsin and Michigan.[274]

In Chicago, several federal cases are currently underway of teenagers being recruited online by the ISIS. Some of them bought plane tickets to travel overseas but their plans were interrupted by US counter terrorism agents, mainly at O'Hare Airport.

In February 2015, authorities arrested three Brooklyn men for plotting to blow up Coney Island. The three men arrested are said to be from Uzbekistan and Kazakhstan, who planned to train with militants in Syria. It is charged that they hoped to shoot police officers, FBI agents or members of the US military and even spoke of assassinating President Obama.

However, it is Europe that has surprisingly been a major hotbed of ISIS recruitment with between 5,000 and 6,000 Europeans having reportedly travelled to Syria to join the ISIS.[275] This information has come from the European Union's Commissioner for Justice Vera Jourova, who believes it is an underestimate and has also stressed that 1,450 of these people are French citizens. European governments fear that EU nationals, who are traveling to Syria may carry out attacks on return to their home soil.

One such person who returned from Syria is Frenchman Mehdi Nemmouche, who allegedly carried out an attack on May 24, 2014. He is suspected of killing four people in Jewish Museum in Brussels last year.

The three attackers (Said and Cherif Kouachi brothers as well as Amedy Coulibaly) who killed 12 people of the French satirical magazine *Charlie Hebdo* on January 7, 2015, were also said to have returned to France from Syria a few years ago. Although both Al-Qaeda and ISIS claimed responsibility for the attack, authorities believe it may have been 'lone wolf' operation.

Meanwhile, German rapper turned ISIS terrorist Denis Cuspert has released a music video that has threatened his country with a *Charlie Hebdo*-like attack. The 39-year-old who now calls himself Abu Talha Al-Amani, has filled the video with horrific footage of ISIS prisoners being beheaded. In the three minute clip, the rapper sings: "In France deeds were done, in Germany sleepers are waiting. We want your blood."[276]

ISIS PLANS TO START CHRISTIAN-MUSLIM WORLD WAR BY ATTACKING ROME

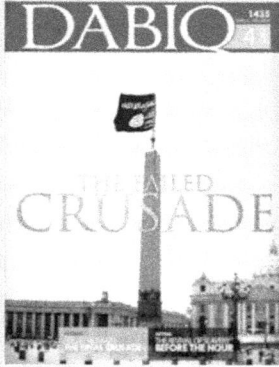

ISIS displays a doctored picture of its flag flying over the Vatican on the cover page of its online magazine Dabiq (4th issue)

In most of his speeches, Abu Bakr Al-Baghdadi speaks of his obsession with the conquest of Rome, which he deems as the seat of Christianity. By attacking the Vatican, the ISIS leader wants to initiate a global religious war or the Malahim Al-Kubra (the Armageddon).

In fact, in many of his sermons, he tells his ISIS members; "You will conquer Rome and own the world, if Allah wills".

The group has already warned the world of its growing presence in Rome and has said that the 'Countdown to Terror' has begun. The group's spokesman Abu Mohammed Al Adnani has said that the group will first target Rome then Paris and London.

The ISIS menace has also been bothering British authorities. In June 2014, then Foreign Secretary William Hague, estimated that 400 British citizens were fighting in Syria, many of them for the ISIS.[277] However, British MP Khalid Mahmood estimated that there were at least 1,500 Britons fighting for the so-called Islamic State. In fact, the ISIS suspect responsible for the beheading of several foreign hostages, known as 'Jihadi John' is believed to be the British citizen Mohammed Emwazi.

Meanwhile, ISIS supporters are claiming on social media that the group has now entered Rome and that the "countdown to terror", implying its planned attack, has started.[278] It has to be noted that in the ISIS' eschatological interpretation of end-times, the group begins a war with the West by attacking the city of Rome.

31. Rising Threat in Eurasia and Central Asia

Central Asia is a mostly Sunni Muslim region and is a "ripe recruiting area for ISIS militants."[279] As the region is still recovering from the power vacuum caused by the end of the Soviet Union in 1991, porous borders allow militants to slip in and out of the countries.

The number of people from Central Asia, who have travelled to ISIS-controlled territories in Syria and Iraq over the past three years is thought to be 4,000.[280] This so-called 'hijrah' has been attributed to the growing trend of political marginalization and bleak economic prospects in five Central Asian countries, namely Kazakhstan, Kyrgyzstan, Tajikistan, Turkmenistan and Uzbekistan.

One of the widely known fighting brigade of the ISIS is 'Shishani Jamaat', which is commanded by the Chechen militant Amir Umar Shishani. Other Russian speaking militant organizations are Jamaat Adama, Jamaat, Akhmada, Abu Kamil Jamaat and Jamaat Khattaba, who constitute jihadists from Chechnya, Caucasus, Dagistanis, etc.[281]

There are a large number of Kazakhs in ISIS ranks. In October 2013, a video showed 150 Kazakhs standing with ISI banner. According to some experts, several Kazakhs are among the founders of the ISIS. In August 2014, Abu Muaz of ISIS's Kazakh Jamaat gave a call to Kazakhs to join jihad in Syria. It has also been reported that the ISIS is behind the disappearance of a 50kg container of Cesium 137 from Kazakhstan, and it is feared that the group is looking for nuclear material. There are also reports that ISIS has a separate Kazakh branch called Jamaat Daoud, which alongside Kazakhs has Uzbeks, Kyrgyz, Nogais, Karachaevs, Russians, Ossetians, Dagestanis, Chechens, Tajiks and even Germans in their ranks.[282] Meanwhile, the leader of the Islamic Movement of Uzbekistan, Usmon Ghazi, pledged allegiance in September 2014 to Baghdadi.[283]

It has also been reported that as many as 200 militants from Tajikistan are fighting for the ISIS. It is also said that Baghdadi has appointed a Tajik member of the ISIS as the 'Amir' of the Syrian province of Raqqa. Similarly, it is believed that about 200-300 Uzbek jihadists are affiliated with the ISIS. A 70-member group called the Saberi Jamaat was said to be led by an Uzbek Abdullah at-Toshkandi.

In January 2015, a video was released showing ISIS militants in Tajikistan calling for jihad against the government of the former Soviet republic.[284] The Islamic Center of Tajikistan warned at the time: "How is it possible to wage jihad in a state whose population is 99 percent Muslim? With whom do they want to wage jihad?"

32. The Spectre in Southeast Asia

The Sunni community in Southeast Asia has been showing increasing signs of radicalization in recent years and signs of growing influence of the ISIS have started manifesting already.

In Indonesia, the most populous Muslim country in the world with majority Sunni population, the government estimates that over 500 people have left the country to join the ISIS. The numbers vary according to who is counting, but the government estimates that more than 500 people have left the country to join the movement. In late March 2015, on the recommendation of the National Counterterrorism Agency (BNPT), the Ministry of Communication blocked 19 websites it claimed to be spreading violent messages and recruiting Indonesians to join ISIS. The move was reversed the next day, however, after a major public outcry, including from civil society groups often attacked by these very websites.[285]

An ISIS recruitment video has surfaced in Malaysia that shows young Malay-speaking boys receiving weapons training in ISIS-held territories. It is estimated that as many as 60 to 150 Malay militants have already joined the ranks of the ISIS.[286] According to Malaysian police, an ISIS attack in the country is imminent. The country's counterterrorism director, Mr Ayub Khan Mydin has reportedly said that, "It is not a matter of if we will be attacked, but when".

Mr Ayub has said that Malaysian members of the ISIS have issued threats to attack the country, including plans to bomb entertainment spots to "punish" Malaysia for being an "apostate" country.[287] "They view us as apostates. First they deem us bidaah (deviant), then they say we are apostates and then next thing is to say our blood is halal (legal)," Mr Ayub said.

The Philippines also considers the threat posed by the ISIS as real. Its foreign affairs secretary, Albert del Rosario has said that the Black Flag Movement in Mindanao has taken 'bayah' (sworn allegiance) of the ISIS' self-styled Caliph.

ISIS is also said to have followers among the Abu Sayyaf, Rajah Solaiman Islamic Movement, Bangsamoro Islamic Freedom Fighters and the Khilafa Islamiyah Mindanao or the Black Flag Movement, according to the presentation of Rommel Banlaoi, Philippine Institute for Peace, Violence and Terrorism Research (PIPVTR) chairman of the board, and director of the Center for Intelligence and National Security Studies (CINSS).[288]

In Singapore, Home Affairs Minister and Deputy Prime Minister Teo Chee Hean said in March 2015 that the growing threat posed by the so-called Islamic State was real and was a threat to South-east Asia.[289]

33.   ISIS in the Indian Subcontinent

For a long time, India has been a "recipient of terror" emanating from outside its borders, but now the threat of radicalization and terrorism is emerging from within its populace, particularly from among some fringe groups of its 157 million strong Muslim community. Although almost the entire Muslim community of India has rejected the radical ideology of global jihadists (including Al-Qaeda and the ISIS), a miniscule number of Indian Muslims have broken bread with some of the most pernicious and violent terror networks of our times. It is particularly disturbing to note that many well-educated Muslims, coming from well-to-do and prosperous households, have fallen prey to the jihadist discourse; which is pervasive and easily accessible on the Internet and social media.

Since independence, India's Muslim population has largely remained patriotic and dedicated to the national cause, yet instances of communal discord and violence in recent decades have festered a feeling of uneasiness and tensions, which has kept the community from fully integrating into the national mainstream and from contributing more substantially to national development.

Several political parties in India have exploited the feelings of disquiet and insecurity spread across all the communities of the country, as part of their vote-bank politics and petty political ends. As these vulnerabilities continue to fester, radical foreign actors have sought to take advantage and pollute young and impressionable minds with messages of hate and sedition.

However, the rise of ISIS has raised the ongoing state of alarm to fever pitch, given its ultra-extremist ideology, its meteoric rise as a global security threat and its dastardly ambitions, which is demonstrated in its map of the Caliphate, which covers the entire Indian subcontinent as part of its imagined Khurasan province.

By broadcasting this message, the ISIS has sought to garner support from the global Muslim community for its unseemly ambitions and the Indian Muslim population, particularly its youth, have not been entirely immune from its dangerous influence.

In fact, within months of the emergence of ISIS on the international stage it was reported that four men – Areeb Majeed, Aman Tandel, Shahin Tanki and Fahad Sheikh – from the Maharashtran town of Kalyan, had joined the group and were operating in Syria. By the end of November 2014, Majeed was said to have returned to India, and on his arrest was handed over to the National Investigation Agency (NIA). During interrogation, Majeed claimed to have killed 55 people in various battles for the ISIS, but had decided to return as he was not paid any money by his jihadist masters.

Officially there have been four Indian citizens (one of them dead already), who joined the ISIS in Iraq. However, according to Iraq's ambassador to India Ahmed Berwari, there may be around 20 Indians fighting for the ISIS, but their identities are not yet clear.

On May 21, 2015, the NIA said on record that the ISIS has designs on India and that the above mentioned four recruits planned to carry out attacks in the country as well. It has also hinted that the self-appointed Caliphate may have developed links with anti-India terror outfits. In a chargesheet filed against Areeb Majeed it said that the terrorist outfit with help from some other terror organisations planned to recruit from India and among NRIs to carry out attacks not just in Iraq and Syria but also in India and other countries.[290]

It has also been reported that the ISIS is trying to upload propaganda videos on the Internet in Indian languages like Hindi, Urdu and Tamil languages, to gain more recruits. It is also curious to note that among its three email addresses, the ISIS' online magazine *Dabiq* has an Indian email address, i.e. *Dabiq*-is@india.com.

There have also been open demonstrations of support by Muslim youths for the ISIS in several regions of the country. In August 2014, two men were reportedly arrested in southern Indian state of Tamil Nadu for printing and selling ISIS T-shirts.

In October of the same year, ISIS flags reportedly surfaced in Kashmir during state election campaign. Then in November, three Muslim youth donned ISIS titled T-shirts in Jharia area of Dhanbad during Muharram processions.

But the most alarming case in this regard was that of ISIS Twitter handler Mahdi Masroor Biswas.

He is a 24-year-old management executive in a multi-national company who worked as an ISIS propaganda activist, tweeting and retweeting thousands of messages.

He is alleged to have interacted with key ISIS figures and with UK-based jihadists. Biswas is said to have 17,700 followers on his Twitter account. The court remanded him for 15 days in police custody for investigation. Hailing from West Bengal, Biswas had admitted to operating "@ShamiWitness" twitter account for many years and used to "ferociously" tweet by collecting information. The tweets contained jihadist propaganda as well as information for would-be recruits and messages praising fighters who have been killed as martyrs. In a two minute 12 second interview to *Channel 4* "Mehdi"

ISIS' INDIAN TWITTER HANDLER

MEHDI BISWAS

Worker at a multinational by day, ISIS' twitter handler by night, with twitter handler @ShamiWitness, 24-year-old Mehdi Biswas has been described by policemen who interrogated him as a genius clouded and confused by fanaticism.

His ambition, it is reported, was not to be a jihadi foot soldier, but to be in the top layers, as a strategist. Although he had never lived in the Levant, he knew extensively about Syria, Palestine, Lebanon, Jordan and Turkey.

He said he was averse to initiating jihad in India as the country has no real Muslims capable of jihad.

had said, "I haven't done anything wrong. I haven't harmed anybody. I haven't broken any law. I haven't raised any war or any violence against the public of India. I haven't waged war against any allies of India."

In early May 2015, an ISIS-linked terror module was busted with the arrest of five men (by the names of Imran Khan, Waseem, Rizwan, Anwar Qureshi and Mazhar) in the city of Ratlam in Madhya Pradesh. According to intelligence sources, the group was being persuaded by its "Syria-based handlers" to target BJP and RSS leaders, apart from police officers, outside Madhya Pradesh. It had, on the instructions of one Yousuf Al Hindi, acquired two pistols and learnt how to assemble IEDs from locally available explosives. The arrested members of the busted ISIS module, all residents of Ratlam, were radicalized over the internet during the course of the last one year. They were being trained on how to make bombs with locally available explosives.

Thus, although the government maintains that ISIS presence in India is "negligible", there is growing concern in the country over its reach among young Muslims via the social media and internet.[291] The NIA is reportedly set to probe the ISIS module.

Meanwhile in Pakistan, six dissident groups of the Tehreek-i-Taliban Pakistan (TTP), led by Mufti Hassan Swati and Hafeez Saeed Khan of Balochistan are said to have affiliated their groups to the ISIS in October 2014. Swati, who previously led the TTP in Peshawar, has been opposed to peace talks with the Pakistani government. His group was involved in unleashing a wave of suicide attacks that killed and injured many people in the second half of 2013. According to Swati, the new ISIS chapter was being led by Hafiz Saeed Khan from its headquarters in Baloshistan. Swati claimed that 10,000 fighters had joined the cross-border group's ranks and training camps had been established throughout the region.

In April 2015, the ISIS affiliates in Afghanistan purportedly carried out a suicide bombing at a bank in Jalalabad that killed 35 people. Although the Afghanistan President said the ISIS had claimed responsibility for carrying out the attack, the ISIS later denied its involvement.

The apparent expansion of the ISIS to regions beyond the Arab world to countries like Afghanistan remains a subject of debate among experts. According to US officials, "while ISIS has dispatched emissaries to places like Afghanistan to make financial promises in exchange for allegiance to the Islamic State brand, there is no evidence of widespread funding or fighters traveling from the Arab world to places like Afghanistan."

In January 2015, police in the capital of Bangladesh, Dhaka, arrested four suspected members of the ISIS, including a 'local coordinator', who was planning to establish a self-declared 'caliphate' in the country. The suspected coordinator, Mohammad Sakhawatul Kabir admitted that the four were planning to collect funds and weapons from prospective supporters. They reportedly divulged their designs by confessing they wanted to attack important government buildings. Kabir was said to having been trained in Pakistan. Police did not say whether the four had travelled to Syria or Iraq to get training from ISIS and it was unclear whether they were acting independently or with the support of the so-called Islamic State.[292]

Meanwhile, the rise of ISIS has forced other jihadist organizations like Al-Qaeda to increase its activities in the Indian sub-continent to remain a relevant threat. On September 4, 2014, Al-Qaeda leader Ayman Al-Zawahiri announced the launch of a new branch of his terrorist network Al-Qaeda in the Indian Sub-Continent (AQIS), dedicated to waging jihad in the subcontinent. The Al-Qaeda supremo said the aim of AQIS is to return Islam "to the Indian subcontinent, which was part of the Muslim world before it was invaded." He specifically mentioned four Indian states, including Kashmir and Gujarat, as well as Bangladesh and Myanmar (Burma) in its area of operations. He even named the leader of the AQIS, as the India-born Asim Umar, who probably studied in Darul Uloom Deoband in UP in the 1990s. In November last year, it was reported that Indian Mujahideen (IM) and Al-Qaeda appear to be working together to launch major attacks in the region. Meanwhile, Ahmed Farouq, deputy head of the AQIS, reportedly died in a US drone strike in Pakistan in January 2015.

34. Operation Inherent Resolve: US-led Multinational Coalition

When the ISIS suddenly burst on to the global stage, by capturing vast swathes of territory in Iraq and Syria in June 2014, the US was already debating its policy of providing military assistance to Syrian opposition groups, many of whom President Obama rightly feared had a hardline jihadist agenda like the ISIS and did not want US-made weapons intended for the moderate Syrian opposition groups like the Free Syrian Army to fall into the hands of the extremist groups. These apprehensions were based on the unfortunate example of Libya, which has descended into utter chaos and divisions following the removal of the Gaddafi regime. The US also faced strong opposition from Russia over its stance against the Bashar Al-Assad regime in Syria and relations between the two countries hit an all time low since the Cold War with Russian intervention in Crimea, following the political crisis in Ukraine in early 2014.

Even after the emergence of the grave threat posed by the ISIS to the territorial integrity of Iraq and Syria, many regional countries, like Turkey and Saudi Arabia viewed the Bashar Al-Assad regime as the greater threat in the region than jihadist groups like the ISIS and pressured the Obama administration to become more militarily active in removing the Syrian government from power.

The neo-Ottoman designs of Turkey to re-establish its historical sway in the majority Sunni region of Syria and beyond, as well as the insecurity among Sunni states of the Gulf of rising Shiite political influence in Iraq and West Asia, deterred the US from taking affirmative action against the rising tide of Sunni militancy in the region.

However, when the extremities of the ISIS' large-scale savagery and the immediacy of its rapidly expanding strength began to dawn on various nations of West Asia and NATO powers, a more coherent plan of action to fight the menace internationally began to emerge. Thus, in June and July 2014, many countries started to intervene with the US beginning to send troops into Iraq in June 2014.

On August 7, 2014, President Obama in a live address[293] said that the ISIS' persecution of the Yazidis, which had forced them to flee into the Sinjar Mountains had convinced him of the necessity of US military action.[294] The President said that he had ordered airstrikes:

- to protect American diplomats, civilians and military in Erbil at the American consulate or advising Iraqi forces;

- to prevent a potential massacre (genocide) of ISIL on thousands of Yazidis on Mount Sinjar; and

- to stop ISIL's advance on Erbil, the capital of the Kurdish Autonomous Region, where the US had a consulate and a joint operations center with the Iraqi military.

The US air campaign was soon buttressed by airstrikes from eight other countries against the ISIS, which was in concert with ground warfare of Kurdish and Iraqi government forces against the ISIS.

In fact, the US has not sent its ground forces in the military campaign against the ISIS and has limited itself to conducting airstrikes; along with advising, arming, training and providing humanitarian assistance to Kurdish and Iraqi government forces.

Then, beginning in September 2014, as part of an multinational campaign against ISIS, military forces from the US, Bahrain, Jordan, Qatar, Saudi Arabia and the United Arab Emirates launched airstrikes in Syria against the ISIS and groups affiliated with Al-Qaeda.

Mariam Al-Mansouri, the UAE's first **female fighter pilot**, aboard her F-16, led her country's mission when that UAE joined the United States and other allies in airstrikes against the ISIS

On September 10, President Obama delivered a speech in which he declared the intent of the campaign was to "degrade and ultimately destroy" the ISIS. Many critics of the campaign complained that the coalition was doing too little too late, as the ISIS had already reached the full possible extent of its expansion and had gained time to consolidate its positions. It has been since argued that only the presence of ground forces – 'boots on the ground' – would defeat and eradicate the ISIS menace from here on.

While there have been no coalition ground forces in Syria originally, the US government has said that it wants to spend $500 million to fund the training and arming of up to 5,000 moderate rebels to function as ground forces against ISIL. Under the original plan, the rebels would be trained in Saudi Arabia and other unnamed countries and then return to fight in Syria.[295] The moderate opposition groups to receive US arms and military training include the Free Syrian Army, which is a coalition of hundreds of smaller rebel groups supporting the Syria Revolutionaries Front.

For their part, representatives from the jihadist coalition known as Ahrar Al-Sham attended a meeting with the ISIS, the JN, the Khorasan Group, and the Jund Alp-Aqsa in order to forge an alliance against the US-led coalition on November 2, 2014.[296] On November 6, a US airstrike struck Ahrar ash-Sham at its headquarters in Idlib. By 14 November 2014, the deliberations between JN, Jund al-Aqsa, ISIS, and Ahrar ash-Sham reportedly failed.[297]

The US intervention against ISIS, unlike previous American combat operations, was not initially given any name.[298] In fact, there was considerable media criticism against the decision to keep the campaign nameless.[299] The ambiguous nature of the conflict, it was argued, would deprive US service members from receiving acknowledgement, let alone campaign medals or several other decorations.[300] Then on October 15, the US Central Command announced that the campaign against ISIS in Iraq and Syria will be designated Operation Inherent Resolve.[301]

Turkey, which is member of the North Atlantic Treaty Organization (NATO), has been involved in the Syrian Civil War since its beginning in 2011. It has been alleged that many jihadist organizations operating in Syria, have used Turkey as an interstate highway to bring in recruits, weapons and funds freely.

In spite of Turkey's strong stance over the removal of the Assad regime from Syria, and its policy of not directly getting involved in Syrian Civil War, its parliament authorized direct military action both in Iraq and Syria on October 2, 2014, and allowing coalition members to use the country's air bases.

However, the Turkish government set many conditions for its campaign against ISIS, namely the setting up of a buffer zone in northern

Syria, a no-fly zone over certain parts of northern Syria, and the permission to train moderate opposition forces both against the ISIS and the Assad government.

During the ISIS siege of the city of Kobane on the Syrian-Turkish border, Turkey drew a lot of international flak for not coming to the aid of the Kurdish fighters in the city. After much deliberation, Turkish foreign minister announced that his government would allow the peshmerga from the Iraqi Kurdistan Regional Government to cross the Turkish border in order to enter Kobani for supporting Kurdish fighters.[302]

Prior to this change in policy, the Turkish government had refused to allow Kurdish fighters or their supplies to pass through the border to Kurdish units into Kobani. Although Russia is strongly opposed to the rise of the ISIS, as the extremist force harbors anti-Russian terrorist groups from Chechnya, Dagestan and other parts of Central Asia among its ranks, the country has been highly critical of the US-led Operation Inherent Resolve as it claimed it bypassed the United Nations and as the airstrikes were not conducted with the consent of the Syrian government Bashar Al-Assad, its key ally in the region. In fact at the very beginning of the campaign, Russian Foreign Ministry spokesman Alexander Lukashevich said that "this step, in the absence of a UN Security Council decision, would be an act of aggression, a gross violation of international law".[303]

Smoke rises after an apparent US-led coalition airstrike on an ISIS-controlled village near Kobane

For his part, Iranian President Hassan Rouhani condemned the actions of ISIS but also called the airstrikes in Syria "illegal" because they were conducted without the consent of the Syrian government.[304]

Even German Foreign Minister Frank-Walter Steinmeier said that Germany would not be part of the airstrikes if asked to participate.[305] Venezuela and Ecuador also opposed the US-led multi-national operation, but surprisingly the UN Secretary-General welcomed the airstrikes, even as he noted that the involved parties "must abide by international humanitarian law" and must avoid civilian casualties.[306]

35. Assessment of the US-led Campaign of Airstrikes

The absence of Western ground forces in the US-led campaign against the ISIS has allowed the so-called Islamic State to continue to operate in a large part of the territory it acquired in the summer of 2014.

However, it would also be important to note that Operation Inherent Resolve has made a substantive impact on the ability of the ISIS in massing further attacks, has helped Iraqi and Kurdish peshmerga forces to regain some of their lost territories, in taking out some of the oil refineries and targets vital for the group's sustenance and in even eliminating some of the group's top leadership.

In fact, leader of the ISIS Abu Bakr Al-Baghdadi has been seriously injured and incapacitated, if not killed as reported by Iranian media, in one of the US air raids on in mid-March 2015.

The air campaign has proven effective in allowing Iraqi army and Kurdish peshmarga forces retake Tikrit, the Haditha Dama and in stopping ISIS forays into Mount Sinjar.

In Syria, US airpower helped reverse the ISIS' offensive against the Kurdish enclave of Kobane, causing heavy casualties among ISIS troops in the 470 strikes carried out in that battle.[307]

On 22 January 2015, US Ambassador to Iraq Stuart Jones reportedly said that the US-led campaign airstrikes had degraded ISIS and had killed off half of their leaders in Iraq and Syria.[308] In early February 2015, Australian Defence Minister Kevin Andrews announced that over 6,000 ISIS militants had been killed in coalition airstrikes and that over 800 square kilometres (310 sq mi) had been recaptured.[309]

However, Jordan reported that airstrikes conducted by its fighter planes had killed 7,000 ISIS militants from 5 to 7 February 2015. If one were to take this figure into consideration than the total number of ISIS fighters killed by Coalition forces would surpass15,500.[310]

However, one needs to take many of these claims with a degree of caution as it is always difficult to ascertain the number of casualties suffered during an airstrike, particularly when there is no infantry on the ground to verify the claims.

On the flip side, however, it has been pointed out that the ISIS has increased its territory in Syria since the airstrikes of September 2014.[311] However, it has been losing ground in Iraq and is said to have lost 25 percent of its territories, from its peak in late 2014.[312]

It has also been pointed out that the US-led coalition has excluded Syrian nationalists as partners against ISIS in the north (where jihadists are said to be the strongest).

The airstrikes are said to have spared the forces of Bashar Al-Assad and have inadvertently killed civilians, which has helped jihadist propaganda among the masses. Several nationalist rebels have thus given up their fight and some have even joined the jihadist cadres.

It is also claimed that since the coalition campaign began, the Nusra Front has driven nationalist forces out of much of their core territory in northern Syria and ISIS continues to threaten those that remain.[313]

36.   Islamic Scholars Worldwide Speak Out Against ISIS

The Muslim community of the world has with an overwhelming majority condemned the rise of ISIS and whether Sunni or Shia, Salafi or Sufi, conservative or liberal, Muslims and their religious leaders have almost unanimously condemned and denounced ISIS not merely as un-Islamic but actively anti-Islamic.

These include prominent Muslim groups such as the Organisation of Islamic Co-operation[314], representing 57 countries (ISIS has "nothing to do with Islam"); the Islamic Society of North America (ISIS' actions are "in no way representative of what Islam actually teaches"); al-Azhar University in Cairo, the most prestigious seat of learning in the Sunni Muslim world (ISIS is acting "under the guise of this holy religion . . . in an attempt to export their false Islam");[315] and even Saudi Arabia's Salafist Grand Mufti, Abdul Aziz al ash-Sheikh (ISIS is "the number-one enemy of Islam").

In September 2014, more than 120 Islamic scholars co-signed an 18-page "Open letter to Baghdadi", written in Arabic, containing what the Slate website's Filipa Ioannou described as a "technical point-by-point criticism of ISIS' actions and ideology based on the Quran and classical religious texts."

For his part, Shaykh Yusuf Al-Qaradhawi and the International Union of Muslim Scholars said the "declaration of Islamic state by IS is a fantasy and theologically void"[316]. Imams in the UK united against ISIS to say it is "evil and does not represent Islam".[317] The Group of South African Muslim Scholars denounced the so-called Islamic State by saying: "A group called ISIS is presently killing thousands of Muslims in Iraq in the name of Jihad. Some media try to label them as Sunni Muslims and propagating as a conflict between Sunni vs. Shia. But in fact, they are not Sunni Muslims. They are Khwarijites who are the Wahabis – so called Salafis, considered as one of the misguided groups by majority traditional Sunni Muslims." [318]

Renowned Islamic scholar Shaykh Abdul Muhsin Al-Abbad of Indonesia said: "Muslims are prohibited to follow individuals whose real identity is not known. The ISIS is a deviant group for committing takfeer and atrocities against innocents".[319] Similarly, Shaykh Muhammad Al-Yaqoobi has stated: "The Khilafah State declared (by the ISIS) is illegitimate... supporting the group is haram (or forbidden) by Islamic law."

Shaykh Muhammad ibn Hadee has declared the so-called 'jihad' of Al-Qaeda and the ISIS as an evil activity. In his words, "As for these people (ISIS, Al-Qaeda etc.) they are only callers to 'fitnah' (disorder and mayhem), and that which they call jihad is disorder and mayhem. Whether they like it or not we say it loudly it is disorder and mayhem."[320]

Imam Omar Suleiman has spoken extensively against the ISIS: "The Prophet (peace be upon him) cared for the innocent men, women and children that belonged to "the other side" even as he suffered from injustice himself and the loss of his family and closest companions. Despite losing

Khadijah (RA) and Hamza (RA) etc. he never became bitter or unethical. Protecting civilians on all sides is also part of jihad. The oppression of Bashar and Al-Maliki does not justify the taking of an innocent life be it a Muslim, Christian, Yazidi etc. So I openly condemn the ISIS and speak out against them for the havoc they are wreaking upon the people of Iraq and Syria".[321]

Another eminent Islamic religious leader, Imam Syed Sohrawardy has said: "I want to create awareness about the nature of their (ISIS') work — they are using Islam, they are quoting Qur'an, they look like Muslims, they pray like Muslims but they are not Muslim. They are deviant people, and they are doing exactly everything which goes against Islam... This is not jihad, this is terrorism... My focus is Muslim youth, yes, but at the same time creating awareness to all Canadians that we condemn these people as strongly, maybe more strongly, than any other Canadian because they are creating a negative image of my faith — they are creating a negative image of all Muslim communities — and they are betraying us."[322]

Celebrated Islamic scholar Sheikh Yasir Qadhi, who is himself an exponent of the Salafi school of Islam, has been one of the strongest opponents of the ISIS. In his words: "The reality of ISIS is becoming more and more clear, except to those who are deluded and too stubborn to see the truth. This group is nothing other than a modern reincarnation of the Kharijites of old. As our Prophet (peace be upon him) said, these groups would have the best of speech, but the worst of actions; they would spread bloodshed wherever they go, even as they think they are the best of worshippers."

"Anyone who supports or sympathizes with ISIS, unsubscribe from my page now. No amount of the evils of American foreign policy (and yes, there is much that any just person will realize is evil) can justify the murderous rampage of ISIS and its ilk. Muslims and non-Muslims; Sunnis and Shi'ites; women and children; young and old - too many people have been murdered in the brutal fashion imaginable. Scholars from around the world are becoming increasing vocal in their condemnation of them."[323]

The Council of American Islamic Relations (CAIR) has warned American Muslims from joining the ISIS. A statement by the organization reads: "American Muslims view the actions of ISIS as un-Islamic and morally repugnant. No religion condones the murder of civilians, the

Why Westerners Turn to Jihadism

Samantha Lewthwaite

A British woman known as the White Widow, Samantha Lewthwaite, is one of the most wanted terrorist suspects in the world. According to several experts, most Western youngsters are getting drawn to ISIS out of a spirit of youthful adventurism, a kind of sentiment witnessed in the 1960s for joining insurgent groups in Latin America and Western Asia. A lack of belonging to Europe among young Muslims of the continent draws many to the ISIS which provides them a sense of readymade identity. They feel they are part of a global movement, a grand project to recreate the world as they know it. Often these youth come from broken homes or a family having a criminal background. The shadow of crime in their past, makes them detached from society and they think that it is against them. So they turn to an identity that the society is also against. In Islam and Muslims they find a rebel identity, a counter culture.

beheading of religious scholars or the desecration of houses of worship. We condemn the actions of ISIS and reject its assertion that all Muslims are required to pay allegiance to its leader. CAIR strongly urges American imams and other community leaders to continue to speak out against American Muslims traveling abroad to join extremist groups and sectarian militias. While ISIS uses romanticized imagery in its propaganda materials, its human rights abuses on the ground are well-documented."[324]

Hai`ah Al-Sham Al-Islamiyah has given six reasons why the declaration of the Caliphate by the ISIS is illegitimate:

1. The declaration of the 'Caliphate' was by a dissident group that practices Takfir (calling people apostates) and sheds blood as religion in and of itself. This methodology is totally perverted from the example of the Prophet (peace be upon him) who taught the Ummah true leadership and how to establish a noble and upright Khilāfah (Khilāfah Rāshida), exemplified by his companions.

2. The absence of the (necessary) elements that compose a 'state', both legally and by what is

understood through custom. Even if they truly had authority in the land and prevalence they would have appeared in person, thus they are closer to being a gang than a state.

3. The unilateral declaration of Khilāfah without the consultation of scholars or the Muslims in general, due to al-Baghdadi's group's belief that they are exclusively the people of Shura while others are apostates or members of 'Sahwas'.

Such unilateral action totally disregards and undermines the authority of the whole Muslim nation. 'The Second Caliph Umar (RA) said: "Whoever gives the pledge of allegiance to a man without the consultation of the Muslims should not be given the pledge of allegiance, nor should the one who he gave it to out of deception, lest they will both be killed." Ibn Hajar may Allāh mercy on him said in Fathul-Bāri: 'This means, whoever does this, has deceived himself and his companion, subjecting both to the possibility of being killed.'

4. The forcing of people to give al-Baghdadi the pledge of allegiance while it has not been given to them in the first place. They said that 'due to the declaration of the Khilāfah it has become incumbent upon all Muslims to swear allegiance to it and to give victory to Ibrahim...' and that 'he has become the leader and Khalīfah of Muslims everywhere!' They added, 'whoever wants to cause division should be shot in the head, whoever it may be without dignity.'

5. The appointment of a completely unknown 'Khalifah' (apart from his name), not recognised by any scholar nor the masses of his own group let alone the majority of all Muslims, completely disregarding the conditions set out by the scholars that form a leader. This is a form of ridicule towards the Ummah, and is similar to the behaviour of dictatorships.

6. The overturning of al-Baghdadi's original commitment of allegiance to his leader Ayman l-Zawahiri. Previously al-Baghdadi had said: "We owe it to God that you are our governor and upon us is to listen and obey as long as we live." Al-Zawahiri had long issued an instruction to abolish ISIS in Syria. Will treachery, betrayal and failed promises be the first thing the "Khalifah" of the Muslims gets up to?[325]

To cap it all, 80 Muslim leaders and intellectuals from India have jointly written a letter condemning the ISIS and its violence. "We strongly condemn such barbarism which is against the teachings of Islam. We express our heart-felt sympathies and solidarity with the survivors of those whose near and dear ones have been mercilessly butchered, and the tens of thousands of Iraq's minorities who have been dispossessed, forced to flee their homes and are now living in extremely difficult circumstances… It is of utmost importance to highlight here that ISIS not only conducts atrocities against minorities, but against everyone who is against their policies, all in the name of Islam. This violence based on the wrong interpretation of Islam is unacceptable… Their brutality is worse than genocide. They are killing women, elderly and children who are respected in Islam. Their conduct is against every teachings of Islam".[326]

In fact, there are several eminent Islamic scholars and community leaders whose condemnation of the ISIS could not be incorporated in this study on account of paucity of space. The organization has only received support from a very small number of Muslims globally, mainly a few misguided youth or neophytes, whose understanding of the religion of Islam is very limited.

37. Conspiracy Theories and 'The Yonin Plan'

The rise of jihadism, with its pre-modern millennial mindset, emerging as a threat to 21st century global security has been difficult to comprehend for many Western minds, ever since the 9/11 attacks. A hitherto unfamiliar sense of paranoia and disbelief has gripped large sections of Western society and even educated and acclaimed intellectuals find the rapidly unfolding events and developments sweeping through the Middle East as too incredible to be taken at "face value".

Thus, it is not difficult to understand the proliferation of conspiracy theories on the Internet and a large audience that find highly farfetched and untenable alternate political theories as the real reasons for events unfolding at the geopolitical levels these days.

Sometimes, such conspiracy theories are promoted even by high-ranking officials and heads of state of governments, particularly in the conflict-ridden Arab and Muslim world, which has long been vulnerable to the so-called "persecution complex".

For example, many Iraqi military officials of the day claim that the ISIS is receiving military and financial aid from the US. Brigadier General Abed Al-Maliki, a senior Iraqi army commander in Samarra says, "Everybody knows that the Americans are dropping supplies to ISIS."[327] He adds that during the fiercest fighting between the ISIS and the Iraqi military last year, US Special Operations forces dropped behind enemy lines to assist ISIS militants. "They came in with parachutes and they were helping to bomb the cities," he alleges. *"It's just a show," he said, sitting in the city's army command headquarters. "If the Americans want to finish something, they will finish it. If they wanted to liberate Iraq, they could."*

The report follows a story run by Iran's Islamic Republic News Agency (IRNA), which cites a supposed interview with National Security Agency (NSA) leaker Edward Snowden. During the interview, Snowden alleges that the US, Britain and Israel are behind the creation of the ISIS and that they have invented the "terrorist organisation capable of centralising all extremist actions across the world". According to IRNA, Snowden has also purportedly revealed the name of this secret operation as Operation Beehive, also called 'Hornet's Nest'.[328] In fact, Iran's Supreme Leader Ayatollah Ali Khamenei has often publicly expressed his views on the relations between US and ISIS.

Similarly, a report submitted to the United Nations Security Council by UN observers in the Golan Heights in December 2014, states that over the past 18 months since the submission of the report, Israeli Defence Forces (IDF) have been in regular contact with Syrian rebels, including ISIS fighters.[329]

Israel had initially claimed that it was treating only civilians. However, reports suggest that members of Israel's Druze minority had protested the hospitalization of wounded Syrian fighters from the al-Qaeda-linked al-Nusra Front in Israel.

A statement issued by a group of Druze activists accused the Israeli government of supporting radical Sunni factions such as the Islamic State (ISIS).Replying to a question by i24 News[330] on whether Israel has given medical assistance to members of al-Nusra and ISIS, an Israeli military spokesman's office said: "In the past two years the Israel Defence Forces have been engaged in humanitarian, life-saving aid to wounded Syrians, irrespective of their identity." The UN report also laid out instances where in Israeli army was seen interacting with armed rebels. In one incident, the report claimed that the IDF gave some boxes to the Syrian armed rebels.

The BBC has reported that many Lebanese people believe former US Secretary of State Hillary Clinton admitted in her latest book *Hard Choices,* that the US had created the ISIS group. "Most people here believe the US and Saudi are one and when it comes strictly down to oil money; the ultimate benefactor from the whole IS debacle is Saudi/the US.

As history teaches us, it is usually the benefactors who are the instigators," said Amer Murad, a native of Beirut. There have also been outlandish claims that Abu Bakr Al-Baghdadi is in fact a Mosaad agent and his real name is Simon Eliot and that the ISIS is the abbreviation of the English name of Mosaad, i.e. Israel's Secret Intelligence Service. As always, the claims are as untenable as the proof is fictitious.

In addition, social media users across the Arab world have shared screenshots entitled 'Password 360', which they allege is an admission by former Secretary of State Hillary Clinton's book, "admitting" the US has invented the ISIS. However, this screenshot does not bear any reality to what is in the book, which is not even called "Password 360", nor is there any mention of such a claim in the book, which as stated above is called "Hard Choices".

Even an employee of the Dutch Justice Ministry Yasmina Haifi, has been quoted in De Telegraaf as saying: "[ISIS] has nothing to do with Islam. It's part of a plan by Zionists, who are deliberately trying to blacken Islam's name." However, the lady later distanced herself from her said assertions.

Most conspiracy theorists of the ISIS connect the rise of the terror group to an alleged Zionist Plan for the Middle East, known as the Yinon Plan.[331] The plan allegedly seeks to reconfigure Israel's geopolitical environment through the balkanization of the surrounding Arab countries.

The "weakening and eventual fracturing of neighboring Arab states is said to be part of an Israeli expansionist project for creating a *"Greater Israel,"* which will consist the Jews' Biblical area, extending from the Nile Valley to the Euphrates. As always, these conspiracy theories are hard to prove or disprove and so they continue to linger in the public imagination, irrespective of their being farfetched and untenable.

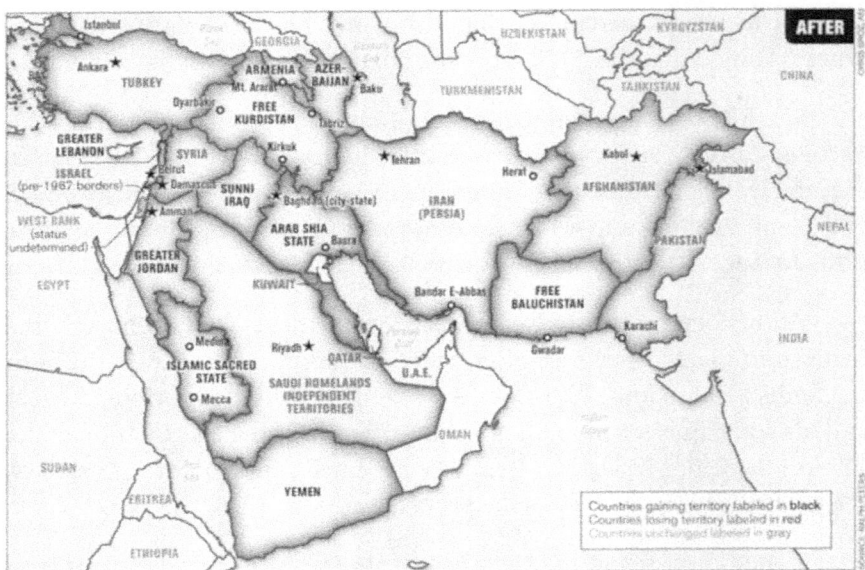

The above map was prepared by Lieutenant-Colonel Ralph Peters. It was published in the Armed Forces Journal in June 2006, Peters is a retired colonel of the U.S. National War Academy.

It is believed that Oded Yinon, an Israeli journalist who was also attached to Israeli foreign ministry, published a document in 1982 titled, 'A Strategy for Israel in the Nineteen Eighties'.[332] In this document, the Israeli researcher suggested that if Israel had to maintain its regional superiority, it must fragment its surrounding Arab countries into smaller units. The document was later known as the 'Yinon Plan' and was remembered for instigating inter-Arab and inter-Muslim internecine feuds in the form of sectarian wars as the best insurance policy for Israel.[333]

Conspiracy theorists believe that the Israeli lobby through the neoconservative administration under George Bush convinced the US into invading Iraq and trifurcating that country into communal and sectarian lines, by creating a Kurdish state and two Arab states (one belonging to the Shia and the other to Sunnis). Ironically, the current US Vice President Joe Biden favored the division of Iraq and drew the Biden/Gelb plan that was endorsed by the US Senate in 2007, but was ignored by the Bush administration.[334]

At times, conspiracy theories can be more than a nuisance and may be used by extremist organization for propaganda and recruiting purposes.

Therefore, it is important for governments and the global media to counter such unsubstantiated and accusatory conspiratorial yarns with effective counter narratives and not to dismiss them as inconsequential speculation.

38. How Should India Respond to the ISIS Threat

There is some merit in the argument that India has so far been reactive to the threat posed by terrorism and that it is high time to act pro-actively, and to think in terms of prevention and preemption to get ahead of the terrorist threat. There is a clear need to develop a comprehensive anti-terrorism policy that encompasses hard security tools in addition to addressing the underlying factors that catalyze terrorism.

By engaging the Indian Muslim community as the center of gravity, the government should launch a major campaign in perception management. It should also redress the community's legitimate grievances related to social justice and sense of discrimination in order to facilitate its greater involvement in mainstream politics and development.

It should also involve it in developing a religious counter narrative to the jihadist propaganda and draw an effective plan for de-radicalizing its religious seminaries and institutions.

The government should also draw plans to promote the composite ethos and culture of India and implement relevant recommendations for the uplift of the minorities, as detailed in the Sachar Committee Report of 2005.

When it comes to warding off the influence of Al-Qaeda and the ISIS, it is high time that the government designs effective intervention and de-radicalisation programmes. The Indian central and state governments need to engage with leaders and members of the Muslim community and devise effective plans of action at the local and regional levels. The Indian central government should initiate public discussion and institute regional conferences to build effective counter-narrative content against the terrorist online propaganda, keeping the vulnerabilities of the youth in mind.

There is a need to work with religious leaders and respected spiritual guides to reach out to youth and teach them how Islamist hardliners threaten Muslim communities. The lack of education and unemployment among Muslim youth needs to be addressed in full earnest and effective programs need to be devised in this regard.

There is also a need to reverse the growing alienation of the Muslim community and strategically located community centers have to be built to engage people of both communities, particularly youths from Muslim and non-Muslim communities, to come together and participate in sporting and co-curricular activities. It is time that schools, communities and civil society campaign against the menace of communalism and extremism in society and improve digital literacy to check the spread of online extremism. The government should also work with Internet companies worldwide to restrict user access to terrorist materials online.

Here the importance of introducing new legislation and establishing new institutions to prevent terrorism in a comprehensive manner cannot be overemphasized. These efforts should complement an effective monitoring and surveillance program of individuals and institutions that support or espouse extremist ideology or are suspected of involvement in seditious activities. There is also a need to look into the issue of Net Neutrality in all seriousness, and at least radical and websites/blogs with anti-national content promoting extremist and fissiparous tendencies in the country should be blocked.

The importance of monitoring all social media websites effectively cannot be overemphasized and measures like 'ethical hacking' and surveillance of the so-called "dark web" need to be considered in all seriousness.

The country also needs to effectively crack down on money laundering activities like 'hawala' transactions and the reported nexus between corrupt politicians with seedy racketeers having links with terror financing has to be firmly foiled and exposed.

The country also needs to consider instituting a separate ministry for looking into the dangers to internal security posed by terrorism, perhaps on the lines of the US Homeland Security Department, which has proven highly effective in stopping a repeat of any major terrorist attack on US soil since 9/11.

Greater attention should be paid to the development of the Army's special forces and commando units, to carrying out intelligence and counter-terrorist campaigns under an integrated command and towards constant enhancement and upgradation of the National Intelligence Grid or NATGRID to collect comprehensive patterns of intelligence that can be readily accessed by intelligence agencies. There is also the need to gather open-source intelligence by using specialist online surveillance techniques from social networking sites, chat rooms, websites and Internet bulletin boards.

As the Middle East and Africa slide toward political instability and disorder, with states struggling to control their territories, irregular forces led by radical jihadist ideologies of Al-Qaeda ad ISIS pose increasing danger to these regions and the world at large.

The international community will need to engage in this ideological war and cannot solely depend on hard power in its counter-terrorism strategies.

It will have to catalyze social movements that are driven by civil actors and leaders in West Asia and Africa to spread the message of inclusiveness, justice, rule of law and democratic form of governance.

Unless this ideological war is fought and won, the damage wreaked by the ISIS in terms of religious and political extremism, sectarianism and fourth generation asymmetric chaos and violence will be difficult to reverse, long after the group has been consigned to the dustbin of history.

Dark silhouettes of ISIS fighters driving into the night near the city of Raqqa

Endnotes

1   Brooke, Steven. "The Rise of Al-Zarqawi" http://www.weeklystandard.com/
     author/steven-brooke

2   Chulov, Martin; Haramy, Fazal; Ackerman, Spencer. "Iraq army capitulates
     to Isis militants in four cities." *The Guardian* 12 Jun 2014, http://www.
     theguardian.com/world/2014/jun/11/mosul-isis-gunmen-middle-east-
     states

3   FT Reporters "Isis: Armed and Dangerous." *Financial Times* 14 Aug 2014,
     http://www.ft.com/intl/cms/s/2/b7f9f982-22fb-11e4-8dae-00144feabdc0.
     html#axzz3G1Mx08qK

4   Sherfinsky, David quotes Pentagon press secretary Rear Adm. John Kirby
     ("… the way four or five Iraqi divisions kind of melted away.)" "U.S.
     underestimated speed, development of Islamic State, Pentagon says." *The
     Washington Times* 29 September, 2014 http://www.washingtontimes.com/
     news/2014/sep/29/us-underestimated-speed-development-of-islamic-sta/

5   Chulov, Martin. "Iraq faces the abyss after its military melts away" *The
     Guardian* 13 June 2014 http://www.theguardian.com/world/2014/jun/13/
     baghdad-faces-the-abyss-after-its-military-melts-away

6   Beauchamp, Zack. "How the US, its allies and its Enemies all Made
     ISIS possible", Vox Syrian Civil War, 24 August 2014, http://www.vox.
     com/2014/8/25/6065529/isis-rise

7   *Dabiq*, Issue 5, Cover Page title

8   Beauchamp, Zack. "ISIS is Losing", Vox, 23 February, 2015, http://www.vox.
     com/2015/2/23/8085197/is-isis-losing

9   Bender, Jeremy, "Here's Where the Pentagon Says that ISIS is Dominant in
     Iraq and Syria", Business Insider, 14 April, 2015, http://www.businessinsider.
     in/Heres-where-the-Pentagon-says-that-ISIS-is-dominant-in-Iraq-and-
     Syria/articleshow/46923277.cms

10   The White House, President Barack Obama, Statement by the President
     on ISIL, 10 September, 2014, https://www.whitehouse.gov/the-press-
     office/2014/09/10/statement-president-isil-1

11 "ISIS is number one enemy of Islam, says Saudi Grand Mufti", Al-Arabiya news, 19 August, 2014 http://english.alarabiya.net/en/News/middle-east/2014/08/19/Saudi-mufti-ISIS-is-enemy-No-1-of-Islam-.html

12 Hall, John. "The ISIS Map of the World", The Daily Mail, 30 June 2014, http://www.dailymail.co.uk/news/article-2674736/ISIS-militants-declare-formation-caliphate-Syria-Iraq-demand-Muslims-world-swear-allegiance.html#ixzz3WRBr71JA

13 "Apocalyptic ISIS beyond anything We've Seen", The Guardian, 22 August 2014, http://www.theguardian.com/world/2014/aug/21/isis-us-military-iraq-strikes-threat-apocalyptic

14 Neumann, Peter. "Foreign Fighter Total in Syria Now Exceeds 20,000, The International Center for the Study of Radicalisation and Political Violence (ICSR), 26 January 2015, http://icsr.info/2015/01/foreign-fighter-total-syriairaq-now-exceeds-20000-surpasses-afghanistan-conflict-1980s/

15 Cockburn, Patrick. "War with ISIS: Islamic militants have army of 200,000, claims senior Kurdish leader," 16 November 2014, http://www.independent.co.uk/news/world/middle-east/war-with-isis-islamic-militants-have-army-of-200000-claims-kurdish-leader-9863418.html

16 "The many names of ISIS", The Economist, Sep 28th 2014, 23:50, http://www.economist.com/blogs/economist-explains/2014/09/economic-explains-19

17 "Statement by the White House on ISIL", The White House, Office of the Press Secretary, 10 September 2014, http://www.whitehouse.gov/the-press-office/2014/09/10/statement-president-isil-1

18 "ISI confirms Jabhat Al Nurah is its Extension in Syria", The Middle East Media Research Institute (MEMRI) 8 April 2013, http://www.memri.org/report/en/0/0/0/0/0/0/7119.htm

19 Rahman, Khaleda. "Boy Flogged 60 times in town square for calling terror group the 'wrong name', The Daily Mail, 12 February 2015,, http://www.dailymail.co.uk/news/article-2951016/Child-receives-60-lashes-town-square-referring-ISIS-hated-Daesh-term-Iraq.html

20 Krever, Mick. "Why France refuses to Call Militants ISIS," CNN, 23 September, 2014, http://amanpour.blogs.cnn.com/2014/09/23/why-france-refuses-to-call-militants-isis/

21 Ian Black, Rania Abouzaid, Mark Tran, Shiraz Maher, Roger Tooth and Marin Chulov. "The Terrifying Rise of the ISIS", The Guardian, 16 June 2014, http://www.theguardian.com/world/2014/jun/16/terrifying-rise-of-isis-iraq-executions

22 Khalaf, Rola; Jones, Sam. "Selling Terror: How ISIS Details its Brutality",

Financial Times, 17 June 2014http://www.ft.com/intl/cms/s/2/69e70954-f639-11e3-a038-00144feabdc0.html#axzz350lIwTdP

23   "Syria Iraq: The Islamic State Militant Group," BBC Middle East, 2 August 2014, http://www.bbc.com/news/world-middle-east-24179084

24   Taylor, Adam. "France is Ditching the Islamic State Name, 17 September 2014   http://www.washingtonpost.com/blogs/worldviews/wp/2014/09/17/france-is-ditching-the-islamic-state-name-and-replacing-it-with-a-label-the-group-hates/

25   Marc Pierini, The European Union Must Face the Islamic State, Carnegie Group, 2 October 2014, http://carnegieeurope.eu/2014/10/02/european-union-must-face-islamic-state/hqw2

26   Khan, Zeba. "Words matter in ISIS War, so use Daesh," The Boston Globe, 9 October 2014 http://www.bostonglobe.com/opinion/2014/10/09/words-matter-isis-war-use-daesh/V85GYEuasEEJgrUun0dMUP/story.html

27   Laub, Zachary and Masters, Jonathan. "CFR Backgrounder", Council on Foreign Relations, http://www.cfr.org/iraq/islamic-state-iraq-syria/p14811

28   Acun, Can. "Neo Al-Qaeda: The Islamic State of Iraq and the Sham (ISIS)", SETA, 23 June 2014 http://setav.org/en/neo-al-qaeda-the-islamic-state-of-iraq-and-the-sham-isis/perspective/16006

29   Translation by Jeffrey Pool. "Zarqawi's Pledge of Allegiance to Al-Qaeda," The Jamestown Foundation, http://web.archive.org/web/20070930180847/http://www.jamestown.org/publications_details.php?volume_id=400&issue_id=3179&article_id=2369020

30   Acun, Can. "Neo Al-Qaeda: The Islamic State of Iraq and the Sham (ISIS)," SETA, 23 June 2014 http://setav.org/en/neo-al-qaeda-the-islamic-state-of-iraq-and-the-sham-isis/perspective/16006

31   Fishman, Brian. "Using the Mistakes of Al-Qaeda's Franchises to Undermine Its Strategies", The Annals of the American Academy of Political and Social Science, 2 July, 2008, http://ann.sagepub.com/content/618/1/46.full.pdf+html

32   Ibid

33   Acun, Can. "Neo Al-Qaeda: The Islamic State of Iraq and the Sham (ISIS)," SETA, June 23, 2014 http://setav.org/en/neo-al-qaeda-the-islamic-state-of-iraq-and-the-sham-isis/perspective/16006

34   "Jihad Group in Iraq Take an Oath of Allegiance," Islamist Websites Monitor No. 8, 17 October 2006, http://www.memri.org/report/en/0/0/0/0/0/0/1910.htm

35   Roggio, Bill. "The Rump Islamic Emirate of Iraq," The Long War Journal, 16 October 2006, http://www.longwarjournal.org/archives/2006/10/the_rump_islamic_emi.php#

36   "The Cost of Withdrawal from Iraq, Foundation for Defense of Democracies," 15 August, 2007, http://web.archive.org/web/20110524071632/http://www.timesonline.co.uk/tol/news/world/iraq/article1782088.ece

37   "Notifying Mankind of the Birth of the Islamic State", SITE Monitoring Service Enterprise, 29 January 2007 http://ent.siteintelgroup.com/Jihadist-News/site-institute-1-29-07-isoi-birth-of-islamic-state-study.html

38   Benraad, Myriam. "Iraq's Tribal Sahwa: Its Rise and Fall", Journal Essay, Spring 2011, Volume XVIII, Number 1 http://www.mepc.org/journal/middle-east-policy-archives/iraqs-tribal-sahwa-its-rise-and-fall

39   Philipps, Andrew. "How Al-Qaeda Lost Iraq, Australian Journal of International Affairs," 1 March 2009, http://www.polsis.uq.edu.au/docs/PHILLIPSHowAlQaedaLostIraq.pdf

40   Arango, Tim. "Top Al-Qaeda Leaders in Iraq Reported Killed in Raid," New York Times, 19 April 2010, http://www.nytimes.com/2010/04/20/world/middleeast/20baghdad.html?_r=0

41   "US Says 80% of Al-Qaeda Leaders In Iraq Removed," 4 June 2010, http://www.bbc.co.uk/news/10243585

42   Acun, Can. "Neo Al-Qaeda: The Islamic State of Iraq and the Sham (ISIS)", SETA, 23 June 2014 http://setav.org/en/neo-al-qaeda-the-islamic-state-of-iraq-and-the-sham-isis/perspective/16006

43   ibid

44   "US Action in Iraq Fuelled Rise of a Rebel", The New York Times, August 10, 2014. http://www.nytimes.com/2014/08/11/world/middleeast/us-actions-in-iraq-fueled-rise-of-a-rebel.html?_r=0

45   Acun, Can. "Neo Al-Qaeda: The Islamic State of Iraq and the Sham (ISIS)", SETA, 23 June 2014 http://setav.org/en/neo-al-qaeda-the-islamic-state-of-iraq-and-the-sham-isis/perspective/16006

46   Ibid

47   ibid

48   "Jabhat al-Nusra: A Strategic Briefing," Quilliam Foundation, January 8, 2013. http://www.quilliamfoundation.org/wp/wp-content/uploads/publications/free/jabhat-al-nusra-a-strategic-briefing.pdf

49   "Syria's Al-Nusra Pledges Allegiance to Al-Qaeda," Agence France-Presse in Beirut, April 10, 2013, http://www.telegraph.co.uk/news/worldnews/

middleeast/syria/9984444/Syrias-al-Nusra-pledges-allegiance-to-al-Qaeda.
html

50   Translation of al-Qaeda chief Ayman al-Zawahiri's letter to the leaders of
     the two Jihadi groups, http://s3.documentcloud.org/documents/710588/
     translation-of-ayman-al-zawahiris-letter.pdf

51   Can Acun, "Neo Al-Qaeda: The Islamic State of Iraq and the Sham (ISIS)",
     SETA, 23 June, 2014 http://setav.org/en/neo-al-qaeda-the-islamic-state-of-
     iraq-and-the-sham-isis/perspective/16006

52   Al-Qaeda's General Command, "On the Relationship of Qaidat al-Jihad and
     the Islamic State of Iraq and al-Sham," al-Fajr Media, 2 February 2014, http://
     washin.st/1lQPHcZ.

53   Joscelyn, Thomas. "Al-Qaeda's Chief Representative in Syria Killed in
     Suicide   Attack",   23   February   2014,   http://www.longwarjournal.org/
     archives/2014/02/zawahiris_chief_repr.php

54   Johnson, M. Alex. "Deviant and Pathological: What do ISIS Extremists Really
     Want?" NBC News. Retrieved 5 September 2014, http://www.nbcnews.com/
     storyline/isis-terror/deviant-pathological-what-do-isis-extremists-really-
     want-n194136

55   Starr, Barbara; Paton Walsh, Nick; Alkhshali, Hamdi. "ISIS No. 2 al-
     Afri killed in airstrike, Iraq Says", CNN, 14 May 2015, http://edition.cnn.
     com/2015/05/13/middleeast/isis-al-afri/

56   "ISIL Makes Gains in Ramadi, Baiji in Stalemate: Pentagon," Kuwait
     News Agency, 16 May 2015, https://www.kuna.net.kw/ArticleDetails.
     aspx?id=2441686&Language=en

57   Spencer, Richard; Samaan, Magdy. "Islamic State fighters 'in full control of
     Palmyra and have entered the ruins'", The Guardian, 21 May 2015 http://
     www.telegraph.co.uk/news/worldnews/middleeast/syria/11619384/
     Palmyra-ruins-unguarded-as-Islamic-State-storms-town.html

58   Lewis, Bernard. Lecture titled: "Israel, the Jews and the Sunni-Shiite
     Conflict," Hebrew University of Jerusalem,   https://www.youtube.com/
     watch?v=THgechURnkU

59   Halliday, Fred. 100 Myths, 2005, p.85-6

60   Halliday Fred, from "The Left and the Jihad", Open Democracy 7 September
     2006. Opendemocracy.net. 2011-04-06.

61   Daniel Pipes (March 1, 2000). "Islam and Islamism: Faith and Ideology". The
     National Interest (Spring 2000).

62   Abaza Hayri. 'Islam and Islamism: Faith and Ideology', Newsweek, 22

October 2010, https://www.google.co.in/url?sa=t&rct=j&q=&esrc=s&sour
ce=web&cd=1&ved=0CCQQFjAA&url=http%3A%2F%2Fwww.newsweek.
com%2Fit-islamic-or-islamist-73961&ei=9LcwVYr7Mcf38QXnmoGgBA&
usg=AFQjCNERxuCTjK_77MbpiU22RX0mkskZoA

63   Al-Tamimi, Ayemenn Jawad. "The Islamic State of Iraq and al-Sham", *Middle East Review of International Affairs (MERIA Journal)*, Fall 2013

64   Maududi, Abul Ala , "Jihad in Islam" pp.65-66

65   Azzam, Abdullah, "Defence of the Muslim lands: First Obligation After Iman"   http://www.religioscope.com/info/doc/jihad/azzam_defence_3_chap1.htm

66   Husain, Ed. "Saudis Must Stop Exporting Extremism", New York Times, 22 August 2014. http://www.nytimes.com/2014/08/23/opinion/isis-atrocities-started-with-saudi-support-for-salafi-hate.html?_r=0

67   Keller, Nuh. *"Who or what is a Salafi? Is their approach valid?"* http://www.masud.co.uk/ISLAM/nuh/salafi.htm

68   Khan Muqtedar, "Syed Qutb – John Locke of the Islamic World," The Globalist, 28 July, 2003, http://www.theglobalist.com/syed-qutb-john-locke-of-the-islamic-world/

69   Wright, Lawrence. "The Looming Tower and the Road to 9/11", 2006, New York

70   Lawrence Wright, The Looming Tower: Al-Qaeda and the Road to 9/11, Vintage (Publishing), August 21, 2007.

71   Ibid.

72   Eikmeier, Dale. "Qutbism: An Ideology of Islamic-Fascism" from Parameters, Spring 2007, pp.85-98

73   Farag, *al-Farida al-gha'iba*, (Amman, n.d.), p.28, 26; trans. Johannes Jansen, *The Neglected Duty*, (New York, 1986)

74   Wahhab, Muhammad bin Abdul. "Kitab Al-Tawheed" https://www.google.co.in/url?sa=t&rct=j&q=&esrc=s&source=web&cd=1&ved=0CB4QFjAA&url=http%3A%2F%2Fwww.islamicbulletin.org%2Ffree_downloads%2Fnew_muslim%2Fkitab_at_tawheed.pdf&ei=OGNYVcyWKYeRuAStpoLYAg&usg=AFQjCNGaDX_p1Ujc-oEZ0pSYoeIMVPiFQA

75   Open Letter to Baghdadi, by Sheikh Abdallah bin Bayyah, President of Forum for Promoting Peace in Muslim Society, September 19, *http://www.lettertobaghdadi.com/*

76   "Second Ikhwan Rebellion 1929-1930, Armed Conflict Timeline Index, Wars of the World, Globe University, https://www.onwar.com/aced/chrono/

index2010.htm

77   Trevor, Stanley. "Understanding the Origins of Wahhabism and Salafism", Terrorism Monitor Volume 3: 14, The Jamestown Foundation http://www. jamestown.org/programs/tm/single/?tx_ttnews%5Btt_news%5D=528&#. VVHFBo6qpHw

78   Wiktorowicz, Quintan. "Anatomy of the Salafi Movement", Studies in Conflict & Terrorism, 29:207–239, 2006, Routledge http://archives.cerium. ca/IMG/pdf/WIKTOROWICZ_2006_Anatomy_of_the_Salafi_Movement. pdf

79   Heit, John. "What is Jihad", Markulla Center for Applied Ethics, Santa Clara University, http://www.scu.edu/ethics/publications/submitted/heit/ whatisjihad.html

80   Although al-Qaeda's main website was shut down after September 11, it was subsequently hosted at various alternative sites, including one run by The Center for Islamic Studies and Research (*markaz al-dirasat wal-buhuth al-islamiyyah*), which posted the al-Qaeda statement.

81   *Wiktorowicz, Quintan and Kaltner, John.* "Killing in the Name of Islam: Al-Qaeda's Justification for September 11", Middle East Policy Council, Journal, Volume X, Summer 2003, Number 2, http://www.mafhoum.com/ press5/147S29.htm

82   Wright Lawrence. "The Master Plan: For The New Theorists Of Jihad, Al-Qaeda Is Just The Beginning," *The New Yorker*, September 11, 2006 issue, http://www.newyorker.com/magazine/2006/09/11/the-master-plan

83   ibid

84   Moghadam, Assaf; Fishman, Brian (editors). "Fault Lines in Global Jihad: Organizational, Strategic, and Ideological Fissures," (London: Routledge, 2011)

85   An-Nabhani, Taqiuddin. "The Islamic State", Al-Khilafah Publications (December 1995), http://www.hizb-ut-tahrir.org/PDF/EN/en_books_pdf/ IslamicState.pdf

86   Hegghammer, Thomas. "Calculated Caliphate," Lawfare Institute in cooperation with Brookings, 6 July 2014, http://www.lawfareblog. com/2014/07/the-foreign-policy-essay-calculated-caliphate/

87   Mamoun, Abdelhak. "Al-Qaeda Rejects ISIS Caliphate an Succession of Abu Bakr Al-Baghdadi"http://www.iraqinews.com/arab-world-news/al-qaeda-rejects-isis-caliphite-succession-abu-bakr-al-baghdadi/

88   Hegghammer, Thomas. "Calculated Caliphate," Lawfare Institute in

cooperation with Brookings, 6 July 2014, http://www.lawfareblog.com/2014/07/the-foreign-policy-essay-calculated-caliphate/

89   Kirkpatrick, David D. "ISIS' Harsh Brand of Islam Is Rooted in Austere Saudi Creed". *The New York Times*, 24 September 2014, http://www.nytimes.com/2014/09/25/world/middleeast/isis-abu-bakr-baghdadi-caliph-wahhabi.html?_r=0

90   Fishman, Brian. "Redefining the Islamic State: The Fall and Rise of al-Qaeda in Iraq", National Security Studies Program Policy Paper (Washington DC: New America Foundation, 2011), http://security.newamerica.net/sites/newamerica.net/files/policydocs/Fishman_Al_Qaeda_In_Iraq.pdf;

91   Atiyah, "Untitled Letter," December 12, 2005 https://www.ctc.usma.edu/wp-content/uploads/2013/10/Atiyahs-Letter-to-Zarqawi-Original.pdf

92   Abu Muhammad (Ayman al-Zawahiri), "Untitled letter," July 8, 2005, https://www.ctc.usma.edu/wp-content/uploads/2013/10/Zawahiris-Letter-to-Zarqawi-Original.pdf

93   Gen. Dempsey's Remarks at the Aspen Security Forum, US Department of Defense http://www.jcs.mil/Media/Speeches/tabid/3890/Article/10239/gen-dempsey-remarks-at-the-aspen-security-forum-2014.aspx

94   Furnish, Timothy. "Holiest Wars: Islamic Mahdis, Their Jihads, and Osama bin Laden", Praeger, 2005, http://www.abc-clio.com/ABC-CLIOCorporate/product.aspx?pc=C9064C

95   Cockburn Patrick. "War with ISIS: Islamic Militants have Army of 200,000, claims senior Kurdish Leader," *The Independent,* 16 November 2014 http://www.independent.co.uk/news/world/middle-east/war-with-isis-islamic-militants-have-army-of-200000-claims-kurdish-leader-9863418.html

96   Neumann, R. Peter. ""Foreign fighter total in Syria/Iraq now exceeds 20,000; surpasses Afghanistan conflict in the 1980s", International Center for the Study of Radicalization and Political Violence, 26 January 2015. http://icsr.info/2015/01/foreign-fighter-total-syriairaq-now-exceeds-20000-surpasses-afghanistan-conflict-1980s/

97   Mitra, Devirupa. "Not Four But 20, Says Iraqi Envoy of Indian ISIS Fighters", *The Sunday Standard,* 21 September 2015, http://www.newindianexpress.com/thesundaystandard/Not-Four-But-20-Says-Iraqi-Envoy-of-Indian-ISIS-Fighters/2014/09/21/article2441406.ece

98   Sridharan, Vasudeva. "Indian ISIS Fighter Who Killed Dozens Returned Home Due to 'Low Pay From Militant Group," *International Business Times*, 30 November 2014, http://www.ibtimes.co.uk/indian-isis-fighter-who-killed-dozens-returned-home-due-low-pay-militant-group-1477306

99 Westall, Sylvia, "Islamic State Flying Three Jets in Syria: Monitor", Reuters, 17 October 2014, http://www.reuters.com/article/2014/10/17/us-mideast-crisis-jets-idUSKCN0I60TM20141017

100 Hall, John. "Syria Destroys Two Warplanes Used by ISIS to Train Fighter Pilots", 22 October, 2014, http://www.dailymail.co.uk/news/article-2803457/Syria-destroys-two-warplanes-used-ISIS-train-fighter-pilots-terrorist-airforce.html

101 Bender, Bryan. "Stolen US-made equipment a key focus in ISIS fight", *Boston Globe*, 24 October 2014 http://www.nytimes.com/2014/10/06/world/isis-ammunition-is-shown-to-have-origins-in-us-and-china.html?ref=world&_r=1

102 Hall, John. " ISIS Family Tree: Sinister and Organizaed Network that Begins with the Caliph", The Daily Mail, 19 September 2014, http://www.dailymail.co.uk/news/article-2761071/The-ISIS-family-tree-Sinister-organised-network-begins-caliph-continues-rigid-chain-command-level-foot-soldiers.html

103 Zelin, Y. Aaron, "The Islamic State's Model" *The Washington Post*, 28 January 2015. http://www.washingtonpost.com/blogs/monkey-cage/wp/2015/01/28/the-islamic-states-model/

104 ibid

105 Tran, Mark; Weaver, Matthew. "ISIS Announces Islamic Caliphate in Area Straddling Iraq and Syria". *The Guardian*. 30 June, 2014, http://www.theguardian.com/world/2014/jun/30/isis-announces-islamic-caliphate-iraq-syria

106 Elroy, Damien. "Rome will be Conquered Next, says Leader of the Islamic State," *Telegraph.co.uk*. 1 July 2014, http://www.telegraph.co.uk/news/worldnews/middleeast/syria/10939235/Rome-will-be-conquered-next-says-leader-of-Islamic-State.html

107 "The Islamic State" (PDF). The Soufan Group. 28 October 2014.

108 ibid

109 "Baghdadi welcomes new pledges of IS allegiance" Al Monitor. 14 November 2014, http://www.al-monitor.com/pulse/politics/2014/11/baghdadi-speech-islamic-state-pledges-of-allegiance.html

110 Sherlock, Ruth. "Inside the leadership of the Islamic State: How the New Caliphate is Run," http://www.telegraph.co.uk/news/worldnews/middleeast/iraq/10956280/Inside-the-leadership-of-Islamic-State-how-the-new-caliphate-is-run.html

111 Lister, Charles. "Profiling the Islamic State," Brookings Doha Center Analysis Paper, December 1, 2014, http://www.brookings.edu/research/reports2/2014/12/profiling-islamic-state-lister

112 ibid

113 Battle for Iraq and Syria in Maps, BBC Middle East, http://www.bbc.com/news/world-middle-east-27838034

114 Allam, Hannah. "Records Show How Iraqi Extremists Withstood US Anti-Terror Efforts", McClatchy Washington Bureau, 23 June 2014 http://www.mcclatchydc.com/2014/06/23/231223/records-show-how-iraqi-extremists.html

115 ibid

116 Ibid

117 Johnston, Patrick B. "Countering ISIL's Financing", RAND Office of External Affairs, November 2014, http://www.rand.org/content/dam/rand/pubs/testimonies/CT400/CT419/RAND_CT419.pdf

118 Zarate, Juan. "Can the US cut off ISIS from its funding", CBS News, 14 August 2014, 6:00 AM http://www.cbsnews.com/news/can-the-u-s-cut-off-isis-from-its-funding/

119 Haltiwanger, John "ISIS Is Worth $2 Billion, And Makes More Money Than Most Of Your Favorite Companies," Elite Daily, September 18, 2014

120 Johnston, Patrick B. "Countering ISIL's Financing", RAND Office of External Affairs, November 2014, http://www.rand.org/content/dam/rand/pubs/testimonies/CT400/CT419/RAND_CT419.pdf

121 Giovanni, Janine di; Goodman, Leah McGrath; Sharkov, Damien: "How Does ISIS Fund Its Reign of Terror?," Newsweek, 6 November 2014 http://www.newsweek.com/2014/11/14/how-does-isis-fund-its-reign-terror-282607.html

122 Ibid

123 Chulov, Martin. "How an arrest in Iraq revealed Isis's $2bn jihadist network," The Guardian, 15 June 2014, http://www.theguardian.com/world/2014/jun/15/iraq-isis-arrest-jihadists-wealth-power

124 Lister, Charles. "Profiling the Islamic State", Brookings Doha Center Analysis Paper, December 1, 2014, http://www.brookings.edu/research/reports2/2014/12/profiling-islamic-state-lister

125 Ibid

126 Al-Khatteeb, Luay. "How Iraq's black market in oil funds ISIS", Special to

CNN, August 22, 2014 http://edition.cnn.com/2014/08/18/business/al-khatteeb-isis-oil-iraq/index.html

127 Al-Ansary, Khalid; Fattah, Zainab. "Kurds Recapture Iraq Oil Fields, Advance on Rebel-Held Towns," Bloomberg Business, August 28, 2014, http://www.bloomberg.com/news/articles/2014-08-28/kurds-recapture-iraq-oil-fields-advance-on-rebel-held-towns

128 Malas, Nour; Habib, Maria abi. "Islamic State Economy Runs on Extortion, Oil Piracy in Syria and Iraq," http://www.wsj.com/articles/islamic-state-fills-coffers-from-illicit-economy-in-syria-iraq-1409175458

129 Johnson, Keith. "The Islamic State is the Newest Petrostate," Foreign Policy, 28 July 2014 http://foreignpolicy.com/2014/07/28/the-islamic-state-is-the-newest-petrostate/

130 Giovanni, Janine di; Goodman, Leah McGrath; Sharkov, Damien. "How Does ISIS Fund Its Reign of Terror?," *Newsweek*, 6 November 2014 http://www.newsweek.com/2014/11/14/how-does-isis-fund-its-reign-terror-282607.html

131 Mezzofiore, Gianluca. "Kuwaiti Sunni Cleric Accused of Fundraising for ISIS Briefly Detained," International Business Times, August 18, 2014, http://www.ibtimes.co.uk/kuwaiti-sunni-cleric-accused-fundraising-isis-briefly-detained-1461641

132 Ibid

133 Dickinson, Elizabeth. "Playing with Fire: Why Private Gulf Financing for Syria's Extremist Rebels Risks Igniting Sectarian Conflict at Home," Analysis Paper, December 2013 http://www.brookings.edu/~/media/research/files/papers/2013/12/06%20private%20gulf%20financing%20syria%20extremist%20rebels%20sectarian%20conflict%20dickinson/private%20gulf%20financing%20syria%20extremist%20rebels%20sectarian%20conflict%20dickinson.pdf

134 Giovanni, Janine di; Goodman, Leah McGrath; Sharkov, Damien. "How Does ISIS Fund Its Reign of Terror?," *Newsweek*, 6 November 2014 http://www.newsweek.com/2014/11/14/how-does-isis-fund-its-reign-terror-282607.html

135 Ibid

136 Johnston, Patrick. "Countering ISIL's Financing", RAND Office of External Affairs, November 2014, http://www.rand.org/content/dam/rand/pubs/testimonies/CT400/CT419/RAND_CT419.pdf

137 Lister, Charles. "Profiling the Islamic State", Brookings Doha Center Analysis Paper, 1 December 2014 http://www.brookings.edu/research/

reports2/2014/12/profiling-islamic-state-lister

138 Prothero, Mitchell. "Islamic State Issues Fake Tax Receipts to Keep Trade Flowing," McClatchy DC, 3 September 2014, http://www.mcclatchydc.com/2014/09/03/238508/islamic-state-issues-fake-tax.html

139 Lefler, Jenna. "Life Under ISIS in Mosul", Institute for the Study of War Iraq Updates, July 28, 2014 iswiraq.blogspot.com/2014/07/life-under-isis-in-mosul.htm

140 Daragahi, Borzou. "Biggest Bank Robbery that Never Happened", Financial Times, July 17, 2014, http://www.ft.com/intl/cms/s/0378 d4f4-0c28-11e4-9080-00144feabdc0,Authorised=false.html?_i_location=http%3A%2F%2Fwww.ft.com%2Fcms%2Fs%2F0%2F0378d4f4-0c28-11e4-9080-00144feabdc0.html%3Fsiteedition%3Dintl&siteedition=intl&_i_referer=http%3A%2F%2Fwww.businessinsider.in%2FIraqi-Bankers-Say-ISIS-Never-Stole-430-Million-From-Mosul-Banks%2Farticleshow%2F38559979.cms#axzz37jcfWCVQ

141 Critchley, Simon. "The Case for Paying Ransoms," The New York Review of Books http://www.nybooks.com/blogs/nyrblog/2014/nov/12/case-for-paying-ransoms/

142 Giovanni, Janine di; Goodman, Leah McGrath; Sharkov, Damien. "How Does ISIS Fund Its Reign of Terror?," Newsweek, 6 November 2014 http://www.newsweek.com/2014/11/14/how-does-isis-fund-its-reign-terror-282607.html

143 Ibid

144 Parkinson, Joe; Albayrak, Ayla; Mavin, Duncan, "Culture Brigade: Syrian 'Monument Men' Race to Protect Antiquities as Looting Bankrolls Terror", Wall Street Journal, February 10, 2015 http://www.wsj.com/articles/syrian-monuments-men-race-to-protect-antiquities-as-looting-bankrolls-terror-1423615241

145 "The Plight of Mosul's Museum: Iraqi Antiquities at Risk of Ruin," National Public Radio (NPR), July 9, 2014 http://ualrpublicradio.org/post/plight-mosuls-museum-iraqi-antiquities-risk-ruin

146 "ISIS Destroys Ancient Cities of Hatra and Nimrud," MSN, March 8, 2015, http://www.msn.com/en-us/news/trending/reports-isis-destroys-ancient-cities-of-hatra-nimrud/tt-AA9vbDt?q=ISIS%20destroys%20Hatra

147 Evans, Donald; Hameed, Saif, "Islamic State Militants Bulldoze Ancient Nimrud City", Reuters, March 6, 2015, http://www.reuters.com/article/2015/03/06/us-mideast-crisis-iraq-nimrud-idUSKBN0M20GZ20150306

148 "ISIS Destroys Ancient Cities of Hatra and Nimrud", Breitbart, March 8,

2015, http://www.breitbart.com/national-security/2015/03/08/isis-destroys-ancient-cities-of-hatra-nimrud/

149   Ibid

150   Morris, Nigel. "Call for UK to Take Tougher Action to Save Antiquities from ISIS," The Independent, 12 February 2015 http://www.independent.co.uk/news/science/archaeology/call-for-uk-to-take-tougher-action-to-save-antiquities-from-isis-10039793.html

151   Drury, Flora. "ISIS Fanatics Summon Crowd To Ancient Roman Amphitheatre Of Palmyra To Execute 20 Men", Daily Mail, 28 May 2015, http://www.dailymail.co.uk/news/article-3099466/Islamic-State-shoots-dead-20-Palmyra-amphitheatre-monitor.html

152   Moore, Jack. "Caliphate Unveils First Annual Budget", January 5, 2015, http://www.ibtimes.co.uk/isis-news-caliphate-unveils-first-annual-budget-2bn-250m-surplus-war-chest-1481931

153   Sarhan, Amre. "ISIS to Mint its Own Currency: Coins in Gold, Silver an Cooper," Iraqi News, 14, November 2014, http://www.iraqinews.com/features/urgent-isis-announces-its-new-currency-details/

154   Gartenstein-Ross, Daveed; Magen, Amichai. "The Jihadist Governance Dilemma," The Washington Post, 18 July 2014 http://www.washingtonpost.com/blogs/monkey-cage/wp/2014/07/18/the-jihadist-governance-dilemma/

155   Goha's Nail, "Manbij and the Islamic State's Public Administration," Jihadology blog, 22 August 2014, https://gohasnail.wordpress.com/2014/08/22/manbij-and-the-islamic-states-public-administration/

156   Caris, Charles C.; Reynolds, Samuel "ISIS Governance in Syria, Middle East Security" Report 22, Institute for the Study of War, July 2014 http://www.understandingwar.org/report/isis-governance-syria

157   Ibid

158   Lister, Charles. "Profiling the Islamic State," Brookings Doha Center Analysis Paper, December 1, 2014 http://www.brookings.edu/~/media/Research/Files/Reports/2014/11/profiling%20islamic%20state%20lister/en_web_lister.pdf

159   ibid

160   "Convert, pay tax, or die, Islamic State Warns Christians," Reuters, July 18, 2014, http://www.reuters.com/article/2014/07/18/us-iraq-security-christians-idUSKBN0FN29J20140718

161   Ibid

162 Otten, Cathy. "Last Remaining Christians flee Iraq's Mosul," July 22, 2014 http://www.cathyotten.co.uk/?p=495

163 "The Revival of Slavery, Before the Hour", *Dabiq*, Issue 4, October 2014, http://worldanalysis.net/14/2014/10/*Dabiq*-issue-4-failed-crusade/

164 Culzac, Natasha. "British women led by Aqsa Mahmood 'running sharia police unit for Islamic State in Syria," *The Independent*, September 8, 2014, http://www.independent.co.uk/news/world/middle-east/isis-british-women-running-sharia-police-unit-for-islamic-state-in-syria-9717510.html

165 Lister, Charles. "Profiling the Islamic State", Brookings Doha Center Analysis Paper, December 1, 2014 http://www.brookings.edu/~/media/Research/Files/Reports/2014/11/profiling%20islamic%20state%20lister/en_web_lister.pdf

166 Zelin, Aaron Y. "The Islamic State of Iraq and Syria Has a Consumer Protection Office," The Atlantic, June 13, 2014, http://www.theatlantic.com/international/archive/2014/06/the-isis-guide-to-building-an-islamic-state/372769/

167 Zelin, Aaron Y. "The War between ISIS and al-Qaeda for Supremacy of the Global Jihadist Movement", The Washington Institute for Near East Policy.   http://www.washingtoninstitute.org/uploads/Documents/pubs/ResearchNote_20_Zelin.pdf

168 Whitlock, Craig. "Grisly Path to Power in Iraq's Insurgency," *Washington Post*, 27 September 2004, http://www.washingtonpost.com/wp-dyn/content/article/2004/09/27/AR2005040209346.html.

169 Zelin, Aaron Y. "The War between ISIS and al-Qaeda for Supremacy of the Global Jihadist Movement," The Washington Institute for Near East Policy.   http://www.washingtoninstitute.org/uploads/Documents/pubs/ResearchNote_20_Zelin.pdf

170 Ibid

171 *Dabiq*, Khilafah, Issue 1, Page 39, http://www.clarionproject.org/news/islamic-state-isis-isil-propaganda-magazine-*Dabiq*

172 "Why would the US want to be ISIS's 'Far Enemy'?" http://www.fpri.org/geopoliticus/2014/08/why-would-us-want-be-isiss-far-enemy, *Clint Watts*, Foreign Policy Research Institute

173 Kirkpatrick, David. "ISIS' Harsh Brand of Islam Is Rooted in Austere Saudi Creed, 24 September, 2014 http://www.nytimes.com/2014/09/25/world/middleeast/isis-abu-bakr-baghdadi-caliph-wahhabi.html?_r=1

174 Zelin, Aaron Y. "The War between ISIS and al-Qaeda for Supremacy of

the Global Jihadist Movement," The Washington Institute for Near East Policy. http://www.washingtoninstitute.org/uploads/Documents/pubs/ResearchNote_20_Zelin.pdf

175 Zawahari's Letter to Zarqawi, https://www.ctc.usma.edu/wp-content/uploads/2013/10/Zawahiris-Letter-to-Zarqawi-Original.pdf, https://www.ctc.usma.edu/posts/atiyahs-letter-to-zarqawi-english-translation-2

176 Fishman, Brian. "Redefining the Islamic State: The Fall and Rise of al-Qaeda in Iraq", National Security StudiesProgram Policy Paper (Washington DC: New America Foundation. http://security.newamerica.net/sites/newamerica.net/files/policydocs/Fishman_Al_Qaeda_In_Iraq.pdfhttps://web.archive.org/web/20040216114823/http:/www.cpairaq.org/transcripts/20040212_zarqawi_full.html

177 Zelin, Aaron Y. "The Islamic State of Iraq and Syria Has a Consumer Protection Office," The Atlantic, June 13, 2014, http://www.theatlantic.com/international/archive/2014/06/the-isis-guide-to-building-an-islamic-state/372769/

178 Zelin, Aaron Y. "General Guidelies for the Work of a Jihadi," Jihadology, 14 September, 2013, http://jihadology.net/2013/09/14/as-sa%E1%B8%A5ab-media-presents-a-new-release-from-al-qaidahs-dr-ayman-al-%E1%BA%93awahiri-general-guidelines-for-the-work-of-a-jihadi/

179 "Interview with Abu Muhammed Al-Maqdisi…Salafi Jihadism", presented by Yasser Abu Hilaleh, aired July 6, 2005, available from www.aljazeera.net

180 Bergen, Peter. "Strange Bedfellows – Iran and Al-Qaeda," CNN, March 11, 2013 http://edition.cnn.com/2013/03/10/opinion/bergen-iran-al-qaeda/

181 Brooke, Steven. "The Rise of Al-Zarqawi" http://www.weeklystandard.com/author/steven-brooke

182 TRAC, Dabiq: "Islamic State's Apocalyptic 21st century Jihadist Manifesto" http://www.trackingterrorism.org/article/Dabiq-islamic-state%E2%80%99s-isis-apocalyptic-21st-century-jihadist-manifesto

183 Atwan, Abdel Bari. "Secret History of Al-Qaeda," University of California Press, 2006

184 Wright, Lawrence. "The Master Plan: For The New Theorists Of Jihad, Al-Qaeda Is Just The Beginning", The New Yorker, http://www.newyorker.com/magazine/2006/09/11/the-master-plan

185 "The Story of Abu Walid al Masri: The Ideologue of the Afghan Arabs," Ashraq Al-Awsat http://www.aawsat.net/2007/02/article55263707

186 Lia, Brynjar. "Architect of Global Jihad: The Life of Al-Qa'ida Strategist Abu Mus'ab al-Suri", http://www.amazon.com/Architect-Global-Jihad-Al-

Qaeda-Strategist/dp/0199326452

187 Pantucci, Raffaello. "Al-Qaeda 2.0, Survival: Global Politics and Strategy," C Hurst & Co Publishers Ltd (29 May 2009) 50:6, 183-192.

188 Abu Nusab Al-Suri's "Military Theory of Jihad", Translated Excerpts from "Call to Global Islamic Resistance", Site Intel Group, http://news.siteintelgroup.com/blog/index.php/about-us/21-jihad/21-suri-a-mili

189 ibid

190 Filiu, Jean-Pierre; "Apocalypse in Islam", Regents University of California, 2011

191 Ibid

192 Mark Nicols, "Exposed: Jihadi Kidnap and Murder Handbook", The Counter Jihad Report, http://counterjihadreport.com/tag/management-of-savagery/

193 Jack Jenkins. "The Book that Really Explains the ISIS" http://thinkprogress.org/world/2014/09/10/3565635/the-book-that-really-explains-isis-hint-its-not-the-quran)

194 Ibid

195 McCoy, Terrence. "The Calculated Madness Of The Islamic State's Horrifying Brutality", Washington Post, 12 August 2014, http://www.washingtonpost.com/news/morning-mix/wp/2014/08/12/the-calculated-madness-of-the-islamic-states-horrifying-brutality/

196 Crooke, Alaistair. "The ISIS' 'Management of Savagery' in Iraq," Huffington Post, http://www.huffingtonpost.com/alastair-crooke/iraq-isis-alqaeda_b_5542575.html

197 Ibid

198 *Dabiq* Issue 1 (1435, Ramadan) : From Hijrah to Khilafah http://www.clarionproject.org/news/islamic-state-isis-isil-propaganda-magazine-*Dabiq*

199 Mortada, Radwan. "Al-Qaeda's 20-Year Plan: From 9/11 to Final Victory", Al-Akhbar English http://english.al-akhbar.com/node/18437

200 Wright, Lawrence. "The Master Plan: For The New Theorists Of Jihad, Al-Qaeda Is Just The Beginning," *The New Yorker*, September 11, 2006 issue, http://www.newyorker.com/magazine/2006/09/11/the-master-plan

201 Musharbash, Yassin. "The Future of Terrorism: What al-Qaida Really Wants" by Spiegel Online International http://www.spiegel.de/international/the-future-of-terrorism-what-al-qaida-really-wants-a-369448.html

202 Barrett, Richard. "The Islamic State," The Soufan Group, November 2014 http://soufangroup.com/wp-content/uploads/2014/10/TSG-The-Islamic-

State-Nov14.pdf

203 "Saddam's deputy: Baghdad will soon be liberated" Al-Arabiya, 13 July 2014, http://english.alarabiya.net/en/News/middle-east/2014/07/13/Report-Iraq-s-fugitive-Saddam-era-deputy-praises-ISIS.html

204 Harris, Shane. "The Re-Baathification of Iraq" *Foreign Policy,* 21 August 2014, http://foreignpolicy.com/2014/08/21/the-re-baathification-of-iraq/

205 Lister, Charles. "Profiling the Islamic State", Page 21, http://www.brookings.edu/~/media/Research/Files/Reports/2014/11/profiling%20islamic%20state%20lister/en_web_lister.pdf

206 Sherlock, Ruth. "Inside the leadership of the Islamic State: How the New Caliphate is Run," http://www.telegraph.co.uk/news/worldnews/middleeast/iraq/10956280/Inside-the-leadership-of-Islamic-State-how-the-new-caliphate-is-run.html

207 Ibid

208 *Dabiq,* The World Has Divided Into Two Camps (A Call to Hijrah), Islamic State Magazine Issue No. 1, The Return to Khilafah

209 ibid

210 *Dabiq,* From Hijrah to Khilafah, Islamic State Magazine Issue No. 1, The Return to Khilafah

211 Lister, Charles; "Profiling the Islamic State", Page 19, http://www.brookings.edu/~/media/Research/Files/Reports/2014/11/profiling%20islamic%20state%20lister/en_web_lister.pdf

212 ibid

213 *Dabiq,* From Hijrah to Khilafah, Islamic State Magazine Issue No. 1, Page 36, The Return to Khilafah

214 ibid

215 Lewis, Jessica. "AQI's 'Soldier's Harvest' Campaign," Institute for the Study of War, October 9, 2013

216 ibid

217 *Dabiq,* From Hijrah to Khilafah, Islamic State Magazine Issue No. 1, Page 36, The Return to Khilafah

218 Ibid

219 Wong, Kristina. "ISIS Now 'Full-Blown Army,' Officials Warn," The Hill, 23 July 2014, http:// thehill.com/policy/defense/213117-us-officials-warn-isis-worse-than-al-qaeda

220 Gurcan, Metin. "How To Defeat Islamic State's War Machine," Al Monitor, The Pulse of the Middle East, October 14, 2014, http://www.al-monitor.com/pulse/originals/2014/10/turkey-syria-how-to-defat-isis.html#

221 Lind, William S.; Nightengel, Keith; Schmitt, John F.; Sutton, Joseph W.; Wilson, Gary I.; USMC, "The Changing Face of War: Into the Fourth Generation," Marine Core Gazette, October 1989, https://www.mca-marines.org/files/The%20Changing%20Face%20of%20War%20-%20Into%20the%20Fourth%20Generation.pdf

222 Gurcan, Metin; "How To Defeat Islamic State's War Machine", Al-Monitor, The Pulse of the Middle East, 14 October 2014, http://www.al-monitor.com/pulse/originals/2014/10/turkey-syria-how-to-defat-isis.html#

223 Knights, Michael; "ISIL's Political-Military Power in Iraq," CTC Sentinel, 27 August 2014, https://www.ctc.usma.edu/posts/isils-political-military-power-in-iraq

224 Lister, Charles; "Profiling the Islamic State", Page 19, http://www.brookings.edu/~/media/Research/Files/Reports/2014/11/profiling%20islamic%20state%20lister/en_web_lister.pdf

225 Dicharry, Nichole; "Iraq Situation Report: August 13, 2014," Institute for the Study of War, August 21, 2014. http://iswiraq.blogspot.in/2014/08/iraq-situation-report-august-13-2014.html

226 Knights, Michael. "ISIL's Political-Military Power in Iraq," CTC Sentinel, 27 August 2014, https://www.ctc.usma.edu/posts/isils-political-military-power-in-iraq

227 Gurcan, Metin. "How To Defeat Islamic State's War Machine", Al-Monitor, The Pulse of the Middle East, October 14, 2014, http://www.al-monitor.com/pulse/originals/2014/10/turkey-syria-how-to-defat-isis.html#

228 Al-Lami, Alaa. "ISIS' Fighting Doctrine: Sorting Fact from Fiction", Al-Akhbar English, October 31, 2014, http://english.al-akhbar.com/node/22280

229 ibid

230 "Update on Iraq's Insurgency: Interview With Aymenn Jawad al-Tamimi," Musings on Iraq blog, July 1, 2014.

231 Ariel, Ben. "Egyptian Cleric: ISIS Didn't Burn the Jordanian Pilot", Arutz Sheva, February 25, 2015, http://www.israelnationalnews.com/News/News.aspx/191810#.VSEUMfmUfVg

232 Anderson, Gary. "Abu Bakr Al-Baghdadi and The Theory and Practice of Jihad", Small Wars Journal, August 12, 2014, file:///C:/Users/adil/Downloads/Small%20Wars%20Journal%20-%20Abu%20Bakr%20al-Baghdadi%20

and%20the%20Theory%20and%20Practice%20of%20Jihad%20-%202014-08-26.pdf

233 Rozario, Keith. "What do ISIS and Genghis Khan have in Common", August 2014 https://www.keithrozario.com/2014/08/what-do-isis-and-genghis-khan-have-in-common.html

234 ibid

235 ibid

236 McCoy, Terrence. "ISIL Beheadings and the Success of Horrifying Violence", The Washington Post, June 13, 2013, http://www.washingtonpost.com/news/morning-mix/wp/2014/06/13/isis-beheadings-and-the-success-of-horrifying-violence/

237 "Document – Iraq: Ethnic Cleansing on Historic Scale: The Islamic State's Systematic Targeting of Minorities in Northern Iraq," Amnesty International, https://web.archive.org/web/20140912161112/http:/www.amnesty.org/en/library/asset/MDE14/011/2014/en/1af20d2f-501a-4d5d-b7fc-b52719e8dfdf/mde140112014en.html

238 "UN Accuses Islamic State Group of War Crimes," Al-Jazeera, 27 August 2014, http://www.aljazeera.com/news/middleeast/2014/08/un-accuses-islamic-state-group-war-crimes-2014827153541710630.html

239 Arraf, Jane. "Islamic State Seeking to 'Delete' Entire Cultures", 8 November 2014, The Christian Science Monitor, http://www.csmonitor.com/World/Middle-East/2014/1108/Islamic-State-seeking-to-delete-entire-cultures-UNESCO-chief-warns-in-Iraq

240 Withnall, Adam. "ISIS Throws 'Gay' Men Off Tower, Stones Woman Accused of Adultery and Crucifies 17 Young Men", Independent newspaper, 18 January 2015. http://www.independent.co.uk/news/world/middle-east/isis-throws-gay-men-off-tower-stones-woman-accused-of-adultery-and-crucifies-17-young-men-in-retaliatory-wave-of-executions-9986410.html

241 Sanchez, Ray. "United Nations Investigates Claims of ISIS Organ Theft," CNN, 19 February 2015, http://edition.cnn.com/2015/02/18/middleeast/isis-organ-harvesting-claim/

242 Webb, Sam. "ISIS Execution: Video Shows Child Shooting and Israeli Spy in the Head at Point Blank Range," Daily Mirror, 11 March 2015, http://www.mirror.co.uk/news/world-news/isis-execution-video-shows-child-5309406

243 "ISIS Video Shows Boy Executing Russian Spies," The Middle East Media Research Intitute (MEMRI), 13 January 2015 http://www.memritv.org/clip/en/4718.htm

244 Brekke, Kira. "ISIS is Attacking Women and Nobody is Talking About It," The Huffington Post, 8 September 2014, http://www.huffingtonpost.com/2014/09/08/isis-attacks-on-women_n_5775106.html?cps=gravity&ir=India

245 Watson, Ivan. "Treated like Cattle: Yazidi Women Sold, Raped, Enslaved by ISIS", CNN, 30 October 2014, http://edition.cnn.com/2014/10/30/world/meast/isis-female-slaves/

246 Havidar, Ahmed. "The Yezidi Exodus, Girls Raped by ISIS Jump to their Death on Mount Shinghal," Rudaw Media Network, 14 August 2014, http://rudaw.net/english/kurdistan/140820142

247 Hopkins, Steve. "Full Horror of the Yazidis Who Didn't Escape Mount Sinjar: UN Confirms 5,000 Men were Executed and 7,000 Women are Now Kept as Sex Slaves," Daily Mail, 14 October, 2014, http://www.dailymail.co.uk/news/article-2792552/full-horror-yazidis-didn-t-escape-mount-sinjar-confirms-5-000-men-executed-7-000-women-kept-sex-slaves.html

248 "Iraq, Islamic State Seeks to Justify Enslaving Yazidi Women and Girls in Iraq," Reuters, 13 October 2014, http://www.reuters.com/article/2014/10/13/us-mideast-crisis-iraq-yazidis-idUSKCN0I21H620141013

249 Malas, Nour. "Ancient Prophecies Motivate Islamic State Militants: Battlefield Strategies Driven by 1,400-year-old Apocalyptic Ideas," The Wall Street Journal, 18 November 2014, http://www.wsj.com/articles/ancient-prophecies-motivate-islamic-state-militants-1416357441

250 Open Letter to Baghdadi, by HE Sheikh Abdallah bin Bayyah, President of Forum for Promoting Peace in Muslim Society, 19 September 2014, http://www.lettertobaghdadi.com/

251 Mekhennet, Souad: "Jihadi John: Islamic State Killer is Identified", The Washington Post, February 26, 2015, http://www.washingtonpost.com/world/national-security/jihadi-john-the-islamic-state-killer-behind-the-mask-is-a-young-londoner/2015/02/25/d6dbab16-bc43-11e4-bdfa-b8e8f594e6ee_story.html

252 "Ethiopia to mourn ISIS Victims", Ethiopia News Agency, http://www.ena.gov.et/en/index.php/politics/item/666-ethiopia-to-mourn-is-victims#sthash.Vs2hUP3p.dpu

253 Battle of Iraq and Syria in Maps, 7 May 2015, http://www.bbc.com/news/world-middle-east-27838034

254 ibid

255 "ISIS Used Chemical Weapons in Suicide Attack, Kurds Say," NBC News, 15 March 2014, http://www.nbcnews.com/storyline/isis-terror/isis-used-

chemical-weapons-suicide-attack-kurds-say-n323636

256   John Cantlie, "perfect Storm Dabiq, ISSue 9, http://www.blazingcatfur.ca/
      wp-content/uploads/2015/05/Dabiq9.compressed.pdf

257   Dorman, Nick; Dyle, Neil. "British ISIS fanatics have built a dirty bomb and
      boast of the damage it could inflict on London," Daily Mail, http://www.
      mirror.co.uk/news/uk-news/british-isis-fanatics-built-dirty-4721561

258   Martinez, Luiz. "ISIS Has Lost 25% of Its Territories It Once Had in Iraq,"
      ABC News, 13 March, 2014, http://abcnews.go.com/Politics/isis-lost-25-
      percent-territory-held-iraq-us/story?id=29625568

259   Bradley, Matt. "Iraq Recaptures Tikrit From Islamic States", 31 March, 2014,
      http://www.wsj.com/articles/iraqi-security-forces-recapture-tikrit-from-
      islamic-state-1427812777

260   "Despite Tikrit Loss, ISIS Still Holds Vast Swathes of Iraq", The New York
      Times, 7 April, 2015, http://www.nytimes.com/interactive/2014/06/12/
      world/middleeast/the-iraq-isis-conflict-in-maps-photos-and-video.html

261   "The Caliphate Cracks", The Economist, 21 March 2015, http://www.
      economist.com/news/leaders/21646750-though-islamic-state-still-
      spreading-terror-its-weaknesses-are-becoming-apparent

262   ibid

263   Bender, Jeremy. "The Biggest Challenge to ISIS Caliphate May Come From
      Within", Business Insider, March 9, 2015, http://www.businessinsider.in/
      The-biggest-challenge-to-ISISs-Caliphate-may-now-come-from-within/
      articleshow/46505867.cms

264   Matthew, Jerin. "FBI Investigating Apparent ISIS Attacks on Western
      Websites", IB Times, 9 March 2015, http://www.ibtimes.co.uk/fbi-
      investigating-apparent-isis-attacks-western-websites-1491041

265   Alexander, David. "Apparent Islamic State Backers Hack US Military Twitter
      Feed," Reuters, January 12, 2005, http://www.reuters.com/article/2015/01/12/
      us-cybersecurity-centcom-hack-idUSKBN0KL1UZ20150112

266   Liang, Christina Scori. "Cyber Jihad: Countering Islamic State Propaganda,
      Geneva Center for Security Policy," February 2015

267   ibid

268   Berger, JM. "How IS games Twitter," The Atlantic (1606), June 16, 2014,
      http://www.theatlantic.com/international/archive/2014/06/isis-iraq-twitter-
      social-media-strategy/372856/

269   Kalkod, Rajiv. "I am a Soldier, I have No Regrets, Says ISIS Twitter Handler
      Mehdi Masroor Biswas", The Times of India, 19 December 2014, http://

timesofindia.indiatimes.com/india/Im-a-soldier-I-have-no-regrets-says-ISIS-Twitter-handler-Mehdi-Masroor-Biswas/articleshow/45567376.cms

270   Malm, Sara. "Have ISIS now established a stranglehold in Yemen?" 27 April 2015, http://www.dailymail.co.uk/news/article-3057287/Have-ISIS-established-stranglehold-Yemen-Terror-group-s-slick-new-video-claims-set-caliphate-war-torn-country.html#ixzz3Yllpkral

271   Hanna, Jason; Tawfeeq Mohammed. "ISIS says it Bombed Saudi Mosque," CNN, 23 May 2015 http://edition.cnn.com/2015/05/23/middleeast/saudi-arabia-mosque-blast/

272   Hubbard, Ben. "Saudi Arabia Accuses 93 of Terrorist Links, Including to ISIS", New York Times, 28 April 2015, http://www.nytimes.com/2015/04/29/world/middleeast/saudi-arabia-accuses-93-of-terrorist-links-including-to-isis.html

273   Moore, Jack. "ISIS Target Africa in New Issue of Recruitment Magazine," Newsweek, January 4, 2015, http://www.newsweek.com/new-issue-isis-magazine-targets-africa-recruitment-and-expansion-318531

274   Goudie, Chuck. "ISIS Present in all 50 States, FBI Director Says," ABC News, 25 February, 2015, http://abc7chicago.com/news/isis-present-in-all-50-states-fbi-director-says/534732/

275   "Upto 6,000 Europeans Joined ISIS in Syria: EU", Russia TV, 13 April 2015, http://rt.com/news/249261-europeans-isis-syria-commissioner/

276   Thornhill, Ted. "German ISIS Rapper Threatens His Home Nation With A Charlie Hebdo-Like Attack In Music Video Filled With Horrific Footage Of Beheadings And Executions," Daily Mail, 15 April 2015. http://www.dailymail.co.uk/news/article-3040269/German-ISIS-rapper-threatens-home-nation-Charlie-Hebdo-like-attack-music-video-filled-horrific-footage-beheadings-executions.html#ixzz3Yrh24IWR

277   Wintour, Patrick; Watt, Nicholas. "Upto 400 British Citizens may be Fighting in Syria, says William Hague," The Guardian, 16 June 2014, http://www.theguardian.com/uk-news/2014/jun/16/400-uk-citizens-fighting-syria-isis-iraq-william-hague

278   Julian, Hanna Levi. "ISIS Threatens Countdown to Terror in Rome," The Jewish Press, 30 April 2015, http://www.jewishpress.com/news/breaking-news/isis-threatens-countdown-to-terror-in-rome/2015/04/30/

279   Snow, Shawn. "ISIS looks for foothold in Central Asia", The Diplomat, 18 January 2015, http://thediplomat.com/2015/01/isis-looks-for-foothold-in-central-asia/

280   "ISIS in Central Asia, A Growing Threat", Tony Blair Faith Foundation,

28 January 2015, http://tonyblairfaithfoundation.org/religion-geopolitics/reports-analysis/report/isis-central-asia-growing-threat

281   Stoban, P; "ISIS in Central Asia", IDSA, October 22, 2015, http://www.idsa.in/issuebrief/ISISinCentralAsia_pstobdan_221014.html

282   ibid

283   "These Groups Have Pledged Allegiance to ISIS," Huffington Post, 12 January 2015. http://www.huffingtonpost.com/2015/03/11/isis-affiliates-map_n_6849418.html?ir=India&adsSiteOverride=in

284   Snow, Shawn. "ISIS looks for foothold in Central Asia", The Diplomat, 18 January 2015, http://thediplomat.com/2015/01/isis-looks-for-foothold-in-central-asia/

285   Asmarani, Devi. "Indonesia Struggles to Keep Citizens from Joining ISIS", Malay Mail, 5 April 2015, http://www.themalaymailonline.com/opinion/devi-asmarani/article/indonesia-struggles-to-keep-citizens-from-joining-isis#sthash.oUXcHVAO.dpuf

286   Liow, Joseph Chinyong. "Malaysia's ISIS Dilemma", The Strait Times, 28 April 2015, http://news.asiaone.com/news/malaysia/malaysias-isis-dilemma#sthash.nHaUtE7n.dpuf

287   "ISIS attack on Malaysia imminent, says top counterterror official," Today, 18 May 2015, http://www.todayonline.com/world/isis-attack-malaysia-imminent-says-top-counterterror-official?page=1

288   Calica, Aurea. "Islamic State threatens Mindanao, Philippines tells Asean", Philstar, 27 April 2015 http://www.philstar.com/headlines/2015/04/27/1448336/islamic-state-threatens-mindanao-philippines-tells-asean

289   ibid

290   Tiwary, Deeptiman. "ISIS Terrorists Planned to Attack India says NIA", Times of India, 22 May 2015. http://timesofindia.indiatimes.com/india/ISIS-terrorists-planned-to-attack-India-says-NIA/articleshow/47378157.cms

291   "NIA set to probe ISIS module busted in Ratlam", The Times of India, 8 May 2015. http://timesofindia.indiatimes.com/india/NIA-set-to-probe-ISIS-module-busted-in-Ratlam/articleshow/47195908.cms

292   "Bangladesh Arrests Four Suspected ISIS militants", The Daily Star, January 19, 2015, http://www.dailystar.com.lb/News/World/2015/Jan-19/284591-bangladesh-arrests-four-suspected-isis-militants.ashx

293   "Statement by the US President", The White House. 7 August 2014. https://

www.whitehouse.gov/the-press-office/2014/08/07/statement-president

294 Carter, Chelsea J.; Cohen, Tom; Starr, Barbara. "US jet fighters, drones strike ISIS fighters, convoys in Iraq," CNN, 9 August 2014. http://edition.cnn.com/2014/08/08/world/iraq-options/index.html?hpt=hp_t1

295 Szep, Jason; Stewart, Phil; Spetalnick, Matt. McBride, Janet, ed. "Syria's 'moderate' rebels say they need weapons, not training". Reuters, October 12, 2014. http://edition.cnn.com/2014/08/08/world/iraq-options/index.html?hpt=hp_t1

296 Riechmann, Deb. "IS, Al-Qaeda Reach Accord in Syria". Associated Press, November 13, 2014. http://news.yahoo.com/ap-sources-al-qaida-reach-accord-syria-190921017.html

297 "Negotiations failed between the IS, Jabhat al-Nusra and Islamic battalions," Syrian Observatory For Human Rights, 14 November, 2014, http://www.syriahr.com/en/2014/11/negotiations-failed-between-the-is-jabhat-al-nusra-and-islamic-battalions/

298 "US Operation Against ISIL in Iraq Remains Nameless". http://www.military.com/, 18 August 2014. http://www.military.com/

299 "US Needs a Name for the Operation Against ISIS," New York. 3 October 2014. http://nymag.com/

300 "Troops not eligible for campaign medal in fight against ISIS," The Hill, 1 October 2014.

301 "Iraq and Syria Operations Against ISIL Designated as Operation Inherent Resolve," US Central Command, 15 October 2014. http://www.centcom.mil/en/news/articles/iraq-and-syria-ops-against-isil-designated-as-operation-inherent-resolve

302 Beck, John. "US Airdrops Weapons to Kobani, Turkey to Allow Kurdish Peshmarga into Town", Vice News, 20 October 2014, https://news.vice.com/article/us-airdrops-weapons-to-kobane-turkey-to-allow-kurdish-peshmerga-into-town

303 "Russia Warns US against strikes on Islamic State in Syria", BBC News, September 11, 2014. http://www.bbc.com/news/world-middle-east-29154481

304 Saul, Heather. "Syria Air Strikes: Iran 'says US Attacks on ISIS are Illegal'". The Independent, 23 September 2014.

305 Koplowitz, Howard. "Obama ISIS Speech Reaction: Germany, Turkey Won't Join Airstrikes in Syria; UK Won't Rule Them Out." International Business Times, September 11, 2014, http://www.ibtimes.com/obama-isis-speech-

reaction-germany-turkey-wont-join-airstrikes-syria-uk-wont-rule-them-out-1685828

306 "UN Chief Welcomes Airstrikes in Syria," Daily Star, Associated Press, 23 September, 2014. http://www.dailystar.com.lb/News/Middle-East/2014/ Sep-23/271703-un-chief-welcomes-airstrikes-in-syria.ashx

307 Vickery, Scott A. "Operation Inherent Resolve: An Interim Assessment", January 13, 2015, http://www.washingtoninstitute.org/policy-analysis/view/ operation-inherent-resolve-an-interim-assessment

308 Smethurst, Annika. "Australian Forces Claw Back Iraq Territory from Islamic State (IS)", Herald Sun, 3 February 2015. http://www.heraldsun.com. au/news/australian-forces-claw-back-iraq-terroritory-from-islamic-state-is/story-fni0fiyv-1227205679244

309 Sreedharan, Vasudevan. "Jordanian air strikes 'kill 7,000 Isis fighters' in Iraq and Syria," International Business Times, February 9, 2015 http:// www.ibtimes.co.uk/jordanian-airstrikes-kill-7000-isis-fighters-iraq-syria-1487178

310 Cantilero, Monica. "Jordan Says 7,000 ISIS Fighters Killed in Three Days of Airstrikes: UAE Rejoins Bombings," Reuters, 10 February, 2015. http://www. christiantimes.com/article/jordan.says.7000.isis.fighters.killed.in.3.days. of.airstrikes.u.a.e.rejoins.bombings.against.jihadists/50872.htm

311 "ISIS Control of Syria Reportedly Exapnds Since Start of US-led Airstrikes," Associated Press, January 15, 2015 http://www.foxnews.com/ politics/2015/01/15/isis-reportedly-expanding-control-syrian-territory-despite-us-led-airstrikes/

312 Martinez, Luis. "ISIS Has Lost 25 Percent Territory Held Iraq US, ABC News, 13 March 2015 http://abcnews.go.com/Politics/isis-lost-25-percent-territory-held-iraq-us/story?id=29625568

313 Itani, Faysal. "US-led Coalition Needs to Rethink Its Anti-Jihadist Strategy in Syria", Atlantic Council, September 29, 2015 http://www.atlanticcouncil. org/blogs/menasource/us-led-coalition-needs-to-rethink-its-anti-jihadist-strategy-in-syria

314 "OIC Condemns ISIS Forced Displacement of Christians in Iraq", Catholic Center for Studies and Media in Jordan, 22 July 2014, http://en.abouna.org/ en/content/oic-condemns-isis-forced-displacement-christians-iraq

315 "Egypt's Al-Azhar Condemns IS Barbarity," AFP, 3 December 2014, http:// www.dailymail.co.uk/wires/afp/article-2858822/Head-Egypts-Al-Azhar-condemns-IS-barbarity.html

316 "Prominent Scholars Declare ISIS Caliphate Null and Void," Middle East

Monitor, 5 July 2014, https://www.middleeastmonitor.com/news/middle-east/12567-prominent-scholars-declare-isis-caliphate-null-and-void

317 UK Imams Condemn ISIS in online Video, BBC News, 11 July 2015, http://www.bbc.com/news/uk-28270296

318 Scholars Declare ISIS Bogus, The Voice of the Cape, 8 July 2014, http://www.vocfm.co.za/scholars-declare-isis-bogus/

319 "Nasehat Shaikh Abdul Muhsin", Bahasa Indonesia, 5 August 2015, http://muslim.or.id/manhaj/nasehat-syaikh-abdul-muhsin-al-abbad-tentang-isis-dan-khilafah-khayalan-mereka.html

320 "ISIS is a Terrorist Organization Explained by Shaykh Muhammad bin Hadee", Masjid Tawheed Wa Sunnah, Durham, NC. http://mtws.posthaven.com/isis-is-a-terrorist-organization-explained-by-shaykh-muhammad-bin-haadee

321 Suleiman, Omar. "Why we Collectively Condemn ISIS," https://www.facebook.com/imamomarsuleiman/posts/819108761442500

322 "ISIS Betraying Muslims, Says Calgary Imam Before Hunger Strike," http://news.ca.msn.com/top-stories/isis-betraying-muslims-says-calgary-imam-before-hunger-strike

323 Qadhi, Yasir. https://www.facebook.com/yasir.qadhi/posts/ 10152426379988300 , 20 August 2014

324 "CAIR Condemns ISIS Violence and Rejects Calls to Join Extremists Fighting Abroad," 7 July 2014, http://www.cair.com/press-center/press-releases/12551-cair-condemns-isis-violence-and-rejects-calls-to-join-extremists-fighting-abroad.html

325 Statement on the Baghdadi Caliphate, 4 July 2014, http://www.islamicsham.org/letters/1892

326 Ali, Mohammad. "ISIS Action is Worse Than Genocide: Muslim Intellectuals", The Hindu, 20 August 2014, http://www.thehindu.com/news/cities/Delhi/isis-action-is-worse-than-genocide-muslim-intellectuals/article6333688.ece

327 Morris, Loveday. "In Fight for Tikrit, US Fins Enemies on Both Sides of the Battle Lines," The Washington Post, 27 March 2015. http://www.washingtonpost.com/world/iraqi-cleric-urges-unity-amid-tension-over-us-strikes/2015/03/27/75bb4f5a-d40b-11e4-8b1e-274d670aa9c9_story.html

328 Baker, Aryn. "Why Iran Believes the Militant Group ISIS is an American Plot," Time Magazine, 19 June, 2014, http://time.com/2992269/isis-is-an-american-plot-says-iran/

329 Ravid, Barak. "UN Reveals Isreali Links with Syrian Rebels", December

7, 2014, Haaretz, http://www.haaretz.com/news/diplomacy-defense/.
premium-1.630359

330 "Regular Contact Between Israel and Syrian Rebels: UN Report," December
7, 2014, http://www.i24news.tv/en/news/international/middle-east/53651-
141207-regular-contact-between-israel-and-syrian-rebels-un-report

331 Afroz, Sultana. "The Yinon Plan and the Role of the ISIS," *The Daily Star*,
July 3, 2014, http://www.thedailystar.net/the-yinon-plan-and-the-role-of-
the-isis-31469

332 Atzmon, Gilad. "The Jewish Plan for Middle East and Beyond," June 13,
2014, http://www.gilad.co.uk/writings/the-jewish-plan-for-the-middle-
east-and-beyond.html

333 ibid

334 Lister, Tim. "Iraq to Split into Three: So Why Not?", CNN, July 8, 2014,
http://edition.cnn.com/2014/07/07/world/meast/iraq-division-lister/

Index